PENGUIN BOOKS
THE FISH COOKBOOK

Megha Patil has worked as an architect in both India and UK, as a journalist and editor, and authored books for children. She has held key positions in central and state government bodies as well as private sector organizations, especially in the area of rural development. She is also involved in working with underprivileged women and children. Among her passions is food, and during her extensive travels, she has sampled and experimented with many different cuisines.

Megha Patil lives in Mumbai and has two daughters.

THE
FISH
COOKBOOK

Megha Patil

PENGUIN BOOKS

PENGUIN BOOKS

USA | Canada | UK | Ireland | Australia
New Zealand | India | South Africa | China

Penguin Books is part of the Penguin Random House group of companies
whose addresses can be found at global.penguinrandomhouse.com

Published by Penguin Random House India Pvt. Ltd
7th Floor, Infinity Tower C, DLF Cyber City,
Gurgaon 122 002, Haryana, India

First published by Penguin Books India 2000

10 9 8 7 6 5

ISBN 9780140294507

Typeset in Sabon by Digital Technologies and Printing Solutions, New Delhi
Printed at Repro Knowledgecast Limited, India

www.penguin.co.in

For Aiee, Neela, Shailesh, Sonetta and Vinetta

Contents

Introduction

Fish is the simplest and healthiest form of obtaining your dietary requirements of protein. It is low in calories and, with the exception of shellfish, low in cholesterol. It contains essential vitamins and minerals but no saturated fats. Fish is generally identified as being good for the brain but this theory has not been scientifically substantiated. It is believed that oysters, lobster tails, octopus or calamari and caviar act as aphrodisiacs.

Fish also has many advantages from the culinary point of view. It is easier and quicker to cook than meat and poultry. The variety of seafood is so abundant that it seldom gets boring to the palate. If a specific variety is not available, it can easily be substituted by any other fish from the same family. It is usually more economical. Fish can be curried, fried, baked, broiled, grilled or poached. The only care to be taken while cooking fish is not to overcook it as it will be flaky and dry, and shellfish will turn rubbery and inedible. When fish turns milky white all the way down to the bone and can be flaked easily with a fork, it is done.

A large variety of fish is available in India. It is available fresh in coastal areas and in most other places. Fresh water fish is widely available. Frozen fish and dried fish are also popular and easily procured. The Government of India is promoting the industry of fisheries and encouraging private enterprise in the field by offering attractive economic incentives. With a vast coastline and variety of fish available in the Arabian Sea, Indian Ocean and the Bay of Bengal, the seafood industry in India is growing steadily.

Come with me to the western coast, along the Arabian Sea. This rugged coastline, rocky or sandy in parts, is fringed with a luxuriant growth of palm trees, and from the womb of the hinterland burst forth aromatic spices, cashew nuts, exotic fruits and varieties of rice. Most of the recipes in this book, many closely-guarded family secrets, are from Kelwe-Mahim coast and the coast between Mumbai and Gujarat.

A quick peep into history gives an idea how the distinctive flavours of this area evolved. The Portuguese were the first Europeans to arrive, when Vasco da Gama landed at Calicut in 1498 and made Goa their capital in 1510. They established trading stations along the coast at Mumbai, Bassein, Diu and Daman. The cuisine of Goa is strongly Portuguese in flavour but blended with local spices and coconut, whereas the cuisine along the Konkan coast up to Mumbai has a less pervasive Portuguese influence and largely retains its local character. The Portuguese owned Mumbai until 1662, when it formed a part of the dowry brought by the Portuguese princess, Catherine of Braganza, to Charles II of England. The food in Mumbai cannot be identified with any specific cuisine as each ethnic group maintains its individuality. Immediately to the north of Mumbai lies Bassein, the splendid coastal city settled by the Portuguese in 1534, whose fort and monuments are now reduced to rubble. Further north, near the border of Gujarat, the traditional occupations are fishing, farming rice and vegetables, and distillation of palm liquor and making fruit wines, all of which are reflected in the local cuisine.

I come from a farming family, originally from this part of the coast though settled in Mumbai for the past five generations. Little has been written about the cuisine from this region. It consists predominantly of seafood, and is a curious blend of Konkani cuisine with its exotic spices mingled with the sweet and sour vegetarian palate of the neighboring state of Gujarat. This food is found only in private homes. I shall be sharing with you some of my family's closely guarded recipes of speciality seafood.

Seafood cooked in the Maharashtrian way is generally marinated in turmeric, salt and lime juice for fifteen minutes before cooking. In certain recipes the marinade may be specified. In a warm climate, leave to marinate in a refrigerator. Palm liquor or toddy are the traditional accompaniments. Toddy and coconut feni are used in many recipes, though the former may be substituted by white wine and the latter by vodka.

The cuisine in different parts along the coastline differs keeping in consonance with the traditional palate of the people in different areas as well as subtle differences in flora and location of rivers, river estuaries and deltas which add to different varieties of fish. To showcase this, I have included a selection of recipes from across the country.

The variety of fish found in the Arabian Sea is abundant. I have selected only the most popularly eaten seafood and mentioned fish available in Western countries that may be substituted for tropical varieties (see Glossary). To make cooking simpler, I have worked out the base masalas first. At the beginning of every recipe, I have mentioned a choice of various fish that may be cooked in that particular dish. Any one of those may be chosen according to convenience and personal preferences.

It is traditionally believed that certain fish recipes are especially appropriate for people of certain sun signs. It may be interesting to keep these in mind when entertaining.

Aquarius	Coconut black masala curry
	Prawns and ripe mango salad
Pisces	Crab curry with groundnuts
Aries	Onion masala fish with potatoes
Taurus	Stuffed pomfret with prawns
Gemini	Prawn lemon grass pulao
	Sweet and sour jawla.
Cancer	Pomfret with green masala chutney and bananas
Leo	Coconut red chilli curry
	Stuffed vegetables with prawns

Virgo	Baked pomfret
	Prawns in whole coconut
Libra	Crab claws in coconut cream
Scorpio	Prawn pulao with baby aubergine
Sagittarius	Stewed vegetables with prawn
	Poached pomfret in feni
Capricorn	Pomfret with onion and garlic stuffing

While putting pen to paper, I have particularly in my thoughts the overseas Maharashtrians and hope they find this book useful. This book is for all seafood lovers like myself and those that are always seeking the birth of exotica in their own kitchens.

Preparing Fish

Fish must be stored in a freezer. Unless you are cooking it immediately, it should be frozen when fresh. You can tell whether a fish is fresh by examining its gills which should be bright red and moist. It should have a faint sea smell but not a strong unpleasant odour.

Before cooking, fish must be cleaned thoroughly according to the directions given below.

TO CLEAN FISH

- Place the fish on a non-slip chopping board.

- Press down firmly with one hand and scrape off all the scales on both sides with a knife, working from tail to head.

- Take a sharp cleaver and chop off all the fins.

- For large fish, lift the flap near the head, snip the gills with kitchen shears, pull out and discard.

- If you want to keep the fish whole, cut along the centre of the lower edge of the fish, about 3" for a small or medium fish and about 6" for a large fish.

Open the stomach with your fingers and pull out and discard all the entrails. If there is roe in the stomach, keep aside for cooking.

- If chopping off the head, insert fingers through the opening and pull out brain and other matter. The fish-heads can be cooked separately in a curry.

- For whole pomfret, make an inverted V-cut at the mouth. Insert fingers through the opening and pull out all the entrails and discard.

- Remove the eyes with the end of a sharp knife.

- Gently scrub the dark lining of the stomach with a spoon as this has a bitter taste.

- Wash the fish thoroughly and pat dry with a kitchen towel.

TO PREPARE FISH FOR STUFFING

- Clean the fish thoroughly in cold water and drain.

- Place the fish flat on a non-slip chopping board. With a sharp knife make a vertical cut from below the head to top of tail along one side of the fish, 1" away from the edge, following the shape of the fish. Do not cut through, only up to the bone. Insert the knife flat across at the top end of the cut. Cut through horizontally over the bone to the other end of the fish, 1" away from the edge as if to fillet it. Turn the fish over and do the same on the other side.

- Wash the fish in cold running water, drain and pat dry. Rub in turmeric, lime juice and salt, over and inside the fish. Marinate for fifteen minutes.

TO PREPARE SHELLFISH

CLAMS

- Clams must be firmly shut when buying. Discard any that are open.

- Scrub them thoroughly in running cold water. Put them in a deep saucepan.

- Add just enough water to cover them and place pan over high heat until all shells open. Remove from pan and store the liquid for cooking.

- Cut off upper open shell at the joint with a sharp knife. Discard the shell. The shell with the flesh is ready for cooking.

- If only flesh is to be cooked, remove it with a knife from the shell and discard the shell.

LOBSTERS

- Fill a large deep saucepan with water. Boil on high heat. Put lobsters into the water and continue boiling until they turn red. Remove from saucepan and cool.

- Cut them in half lengthwise, and remove the flesh from the shell. Cube the flesh. It is now ready for cooking. Preserve the shell if you wish to serve in it.

MUSSELS

- Mussels must be firmly shut when buying. Discard any that are open.

- Scrub the mussels with a brush. Wash in running cold water.
- If only the flesh is to be cooked, leave the cleaned mussels in boiling water till they open. Carefully remove flesh from the shell with a knife. Store the liquid for cooking.

OYSTERS

- Oysters must be firmly shut when buying.
- Prise open the oysters with an oyster knife. Remove from the shell with a sharp knife. Feel with your fingers and, with a knife, remove the stone near the fringe.

SHRIMPS AND PRAWNS

- To cook without the shell, take off the head and tail. Remove the shell by prising open lengthwise with your fingers.
- Make a sharp shallow cut with a knife all along the upper length and remove black thread.
- Wash in running cold water.

CRABS

- Crabs must be alive when bought. Ensure that both claws are tied and closed firmly with twine when buying.
- Place the crab on a non-slip chopping board and pressing gently on the shell with one hand, pull at each claw with a brisk tug and sever them from the

body. Pull out the legs and save for cooking. Take off the top shell and discard the eyes. Preserve the shell for cooking as it often contains roe under it.

- Remove and discard spongy mass on the body. Turn the crab over. You will find a diamond shape on the body. Press on it and pull out the diamond-shaped shell. Clean all the sand and waste under it.

- Slice the crab vertically into two halves with a sharp knife.

- Wash all the parts thoroughly with a brush in running cold water.

TO PREPARE AND COOK DRIED FISH

- Dried fish should be soaked in cold water for five to ten minutes and thoroughly washed to remove any traces of sand.

- Cook the dried fish in pieces, or whole if it is shrimps.

- If the dried fish is heavily salted, take care not to add salt to the masala.

- Dried Bombay duck and larger fish can be toasted over charcoal or grilled and eaten with rice and fresh spring onion.

TO PREPARE FISH-HEADS

- Remove gills and eyes.

- Clean thoroughly. Wash in cold water and drain.

- The fleshy parts should be left intact.

Base Masalas

HIRWA WATAN

Green Masala

Makes 1 cupful

1 bunch coriander leaves, chopped
2 green chillies, chopped
1" piece fresh ginger, peeled and diced
6 cloves garlic, peeled and diced
2 tbsp freshly grated or desiccated coconut

- Combine all ingredients.
- Add some water. Grind in an electric mixer or with a hand grinder to thick chutney consistency.
- Store in a refrigerator. Can be stored for upto 3 days.

NARLACHE LAL WATAN

Coconut Red Chilli Masala

Makes 1 cupful

6 large dried red chillies, deseeded and chopped
1" piece ginger, peeled and roughly diced
6 cloves garlic, peeled and diced
2 tbsp freshly grated or desiccated coconut
1" piece cinnamon, broken into bits
2 cloves
¼ tsp cardamom powder
¼ tsp coriander powder
¼ tsp cumin powder
½ tsp aniseed powder
1 pinch mace or nutmeg powder

- Combine all ingredients.

- Add some water. Grind in an electric mixer or with a hand grinder to thick chutney consistency.

- Store in a refrigerator. Can be stored for upto 3 days.

NARLACHE KALE WATAN

Coconut Black Masala

Makes 1 cupful

1 tbsp oil
1 tsp grated ginger
1 tsp minced garlic
1 heaped tsp freshly ground black pepper
¼ tsp cardamom powder
¼ tsp coriander powder
¼ tsp cumin powder
4 tbsp freshly grated or desiccated coconut

- Place flat-bottomed pan on medium heat and add oil.

- Before oil starts to smoke, add all other ingredients except coconut.

- Fry for a minute.

- Add coconut and fry till it starts turning light brown. Turn off heat.

- Cool and store in a refrigerator. Can be stored for upto 3 days.

Curries

Curries

CHINCHECHA KALWAN

Tamarind-Base Curry

Serves 4

This curry has a rich brown colour. Fish that may be used are gol fish, pala, Bombay duck, bangda, boi, whitebait, surmai, rawas, mandeli, pomfret and dried shrimp. Vegetables that may be used are okra or drumsticks or aubergines or large cucumbers.

750 gm fish steaks, cleaned. If using boi, whitebait, mandeli or shrimp, clean and leave whole.

For marinade:

1 level tsp turmeric powder
½ tsp chilli powder
1 tbsp lime juice
½ tsp salt

For ground masala:

1 bunch coriander leaves, chopped
2 green chillies, chopped
1" piece fresh ginger, peeled and roughly diced
6 cloves garlic, peeled and diced

1 tbsp oil
500 gm vegetables, cleaned and chopped
1 tbsp tamarind purée
1 medium tomato
¼ tsp garam masala powder
½ tsp sugar
Salt to taste

- Mix ingredients for marinade, rub into fish and marinate for 15 minutes.

- To peel tomato, put it in boiling water for 3 minutes. Remove and put in cold water or hold under running cold water tap. Peel off the skin. Chop and set aside.

- Mix all ingredients for masala, add some water and grind together in an electric mixer or with a hand grinder to a chutney consistency. Set aside in bowl.

- Place flat-bottomed pan on medium heat and add oil. Before oil starts to smoke, add ground masala and fry lightly, ensuring that green colour is retained. Put in vegetables. Add 1 cup water. Bring to boil, then lower heat. Cover pan with lid and simmer.

- When vegetables are nearly cooked, add tamarind, tomatoes and marinated fish along with all the marinade, 1 cup water, sugar and salt. Cover and cook for 10 minutes or until fish is done.

- Add garam masala, take pan off heat and keep covered for 2 minutes.

- Serve with freshly steamed rice.

WATNACHA KALWAN

Green Curry

Serves 4

This curry has a fresh green colour. Fish that may be used are pomfret, surmai, rawas, pala, Bombay duck, whitebait, mandeli, shrimp, prawn and lobster. No vegetables are added unless cooking shellfish, when potatoes are added.

750 gm fish steaks, cleaned. If using whitebait, mandeli or shellfish, clean and leave whole.

For marinade:

1 level tsp turmeric powder
1 tbsp lime juice
½ tsp salt

1 tbsp oil
1 cup green masala (see p. 3)
½ tsp sugar
¼ tsp gram masala powder
Salt to taste
Lime wedges, to garnish

For shellfish:

1 medium potato, peeled and chopped

- Mix ingredients for marinade, rub into fish and marinate for 15 minutes.

- Place flat-bottomed pan on medium heat and add oil. Before oil starts to smoke, add green masala. Fry lightly, ensuring that green colour is retained and coconut does not burn and turn brown. If cooking shellfish, add chopped potatoes with 2 cups water.

- Bring to boil. Lower heat, cover pan with lid and simmer. When potatoes are nearly cooked, add marinated fish along with all the marinade, 1 cup water, sugar and salt. Cover and cook for 10 minutes or until fish is done.

- Add garam masala, turn off heat and keep covered for 2 minutes.

- Garnish with lime wedges. Serve with freshly steamed rice and koshimbir.

LAL KALWAN

Coconut Red Chilli Curry

Serves 4

This curry has a flame-red colour. Fish that may be used are pomfret, bangda, boi, shrimp, prawn, lobster and crab. No vegetables are added unless cooking shellfish, when potatoes are added.

750 gm fish steaks, cleaned. If using shrimps or prawns, clean and leave whole.

For marinade:

1 level tsp turmeric powder
1 tbsp lime juice
½ tsp salt

1 tbsp oil
1 cup coconut red chilli masala (see p. 4)
4 pods amsul, soaked in 1 tbsp water
½ tsp sugar
Salt to taste

For shellfish:

1 medium potato, peeled and cubed

- Mix ingredients for marinade, rub into fish and marinate for 15 minutes.
- Place flat-bottomed pan on medium heat and add cil. Before oil starts to smoke, add coconut red chilli masala and fry lightly, ensuring that bright red

colour is retained and coconut does not burn and turn brown. If cooking shellfish, put in chopped potatoes with 1 cup water.

- Bring to boil, then lower heat. Cover pan with lid and simmer. When potatoes are nearly cooked, add marinated fish along with the marinade. Add amsul along with water in which it was soaked, lime juice, 1 cup water, sugar and salt. Cover and cook for 10 minutes or until fish is done.

- Serve with freshly steamed rice and koshimbir.

KALYA MASALYACHE KALWAN

Coconut Black Masala Curry

Serves 4

This curry has a dark colour. Fish that may be used are pomfret, surmai, rawas, gol fish, pala, mandeli, karandi, jawla, shrimp, prawn, crab, lobster, oyster, clam and mussel.

> 750 gm fish steaks, cleaned. If using oysters, take off the shell. If using clams and mussels, leave on shell.

For marinade:

> 1 tsp turmeric powder
> 1 tsp lime juice
> ½ tsp salt

> 1 tbsp oil
> 1 cup coconut black masala (see p. 5)
> 1 tsp lime juice
> ½ tsp sugar
> ¼ tsp garam masala powder
> Salt to taste

- Mix ingredients for marinade, rub into fish and marinate for 15 minutes.

- Heat oil on medium heat in flat-bottomed pan. Add coconut black masala. Add 2 cups water, lime juice, sugar and salt and bring to boil.

- Lower heat. Add marinated fish along with all the marinade and some water if necessary. Cover pan with lid and cook for 10 minutes or until fish is done. Do not overcook shellfish or it will turn rubbery.

- Add garam masala. Turn off heat and keep covered for 2 minutes.

- Serve with freshly steamed rice and spring onion.

CHIMBORICHE KALWAN

Crab Curry

Serves 2-3

4 medium or 8 small crabs, cleaned and prepared.

For marinade:

1 bunch coriander leaves, chopped
4 green chillies, chopped
10 cloves garlic, peeled and chopped
2 tbsp chopped ginger
1 tsp turmeric powder
2 tbsp lime juice
½ tsp salt

4 tbsp oil
1" piece cinnamon
6 cloves
2 large onions, chopped
2 tbsp freshly ground black pepper
1 tsp cardamom powder
1 tsp coriander powder
1 tsp cumin powder
½ tsp chilli powder
1 tsp turmeric powder
4 cups desiccated coconut
2 cups freshly grated coconut
1 tsp garam masala powder
Salt to taste

- Grind all ingredients for the marinade with some water in an electric mixer or with a hand grinder to a chutney consistency.

- Rub in mixture on the body and claws of the crabs and marinate for 15 minutes.

- Put the legs of the crab in an electric mixer, add water and grind to fine paste. Sieve paste through muslin cloth and extract particle-free juice. Keep juice in bowl.

- Place flat-bottomed pan on medium heat and add oil. Before oil starts to smoke, add cinnamon and cloves. When spices start to splutter, add chopped onion and fry until golden brown. Add black pepper and all powdered spices. Fry for 1 minute. Add desiccated coconut. Fry for 2 minutes till coconut turns brown.

- Add fresh coconut, crabs along with marinade and juice extracted from the crab legs. Add 4 cups water, cover and simmer for 20 minutes till the flesh of crabs turns opaque. Remove from heat, add garam masala and cover for 2 minutes.

- This curry tastes best when stored overnight and eaten the following day.

- Serve with spring onions and freshly steamed rice or with steamed rice cakes.

CHIMBORI SHENGDANYACHE KALWAN

Crab Curry with Groundnuts

Serves 2-3

4 medium or 8 small crabs, cleaned and prepared.

For marinade:

1 tsp turmeric powder
1 tbsp lime juice
½ tsp salt

4 tbsp oil
1 large onion, chopped
2 cups groundnuts, roughly pounded and roasted
1 large tomato, peeled (see p. 10) and diced
1 tsp grated ginger
1 tbsp finely chopped garlic
1 tsp cardamom powder
1 tsp coriander powder
1 tsp cumin powder
1 tsp aniseed powder
2 tsp chilli powder
1 tsp turmeric powder
2 tbsp lime juice
1 tsp garam masala powder
2 tsp sugar
½ cup toddy or coconut feni
Salt to taste

- Mix ingredients for marinade, rub into crabs and marinate for 15 minutes.

- Place flat-bottomed pan on medium heat and add oil. Before oil starts to smoke, add onion and fry until golden brown. Add groundnuts and fry for 2 minutes. Add rest of the ingredients, except toddy or feni and crabs, and fry for 3 minutes. Add 4 cups water, cover and cook for 5 minutes.

- Add marinated crabs and marinade along with some water if necessary. Cover and cook for 20 minutes until flesh of crabs is opaque. Remove from fire, add toddy or feni and keep covered for 2 minutes.

- Serve with spring onions and freshly steamed rice or with steamed rice cakes.

NARLACHÉ KALWAN

Coconut Milk Curry

Serves 4

This curry has a delicate yellow colour. Fish that may be used are prawn, karandi, lobster and shelled oyster. Fruit that may be used are mango, pineapple or bilimb.

750 gm fish, cleaned.

For marinade:

1 level tsp turmeric powder
1 tbsp lime juice
½ tap salt

1 tbsp oil
2 whole green chillies, slit longitudinally
200 gm cashewnuts
½ tsp grated ginger
½ tsp finely chopped garlic
¼ tsp cardamom powder
¼ tsp coriander powder
¼ tsp cumin powder
¼ tsp aniseed powder
2 heaped tbsp raw mango, peeled and cubed
or 2 bilimb, quartered
or 2 heaped tbsp fresh or tinned pineapple
½ tsp sugar
1 heaped tsp rice flour
1 cup coconut milk of medium consistency
1 drop kevda essence or 1 pinch mace or nutmeg powder
Salt to taste

- Mix ingredients for marinade, rub into fish and marinate for 15 minutes.

- Place flat-bottomed pan on medium heat and add oil. Before oil starts to smoke, add chillies, cashewnuts, ginger, garlic, powdered spices and the fruit. Fry for 2 minutes. Add 2 cups water and bring to boil.

- Lower heat and add marinated fish along with marinade, sugar and salt. Cover and cook for 10 minutes.

- With some water, make a smooth paste of the rice flour. Add coconut milk and rice flour paste. Add more water if necessary. Cook for 5 minutes, stirring constantly to ensure that flour does not coagulate and form granules. Remove from heat and add kevda essence or mace or nutmeg powder. Keep covered for 2 minutes.

- Serve with spring onions and freshly steamed rice or steamed rice cakes.

SHEVLATLI KOLAMBI

Shevala and Kakda with Prawn

Serves 4

Shevala and kakda are delicious vegetables, available only in coastal Maharashtra. Shevalas are stalk-like in appearance and kakdas are round fruits with large pips in the centre.

2 cups small fresh or dried prawns, cleaned and prepared. If using dried prawns, soak in water for 10 minutes.

For marinade:

1" piece ginger, peeled and diced
8 cloves garlic, peeled and diced
1 bunch coriander, chopped
2 green chillies, chopped
½ tsp turmeric powder
½ tsp salt

2 bunches shevala (prepared one day prior to cooking)
4 tbsp oil
20 kakdas
3 large onions, chopped fine
1 cup desiccated coconut
1 tsp chilli powder
1 tsp coriander powder
1 tsp cumin powder
½ tsp turmeric powder
½ tsp garam masala powder
1 tbsp crushed jaggery
2 tbsp tamarind purée
2 cups coconut milk of medium consistency
Salt to taste

- Prepare the shevalas one day prior to cooking. Wash and remove outer skin. Cut off and discard yellow top portion of inner stalk. With sharp knife, finely dice rest of stalk. Wash and soak in cold salted water. Refrigerate overnight.

- Grind all ingredients for marinade in an electric mixer or with a hand grinder with some water to a thick consistency. Rub marinade into the prawns. Keep for 15 minutes.

- Place frying pan on medium heat and add 1 tbsp oil. Fry marinated prawns along with marinade for 10 minutes till prawns are done. Set aside.

- Remove stems from kakdas. Pare with sharp knife. Discard pip and mince fine in an electric mixer or with a hand grinder.

- Drain refrigerated shevalas.

- Place flat-bottomed pan on medium heat and add 3 tbsp oil. Before oil starts to smoke, add onion and fry until brown. Add shevalas and kakdas and fry well on low heat for 15 minutes, stirring constantly.

- Add desiccated coconut, powdered spices and jaggery. Fry for 5 minutes stirring constantly. Add fried prawns along with its masala, mix and fry for 5 minutes.

- Add tamarind and fry for 5 minutes. Add coconut milk and bring to boil. Turn off heat immediately.

- Serve hot in bowls with chapati or bhakri. May also be eaten with steamed rice.

MACHHI ANI PANEER CHI AMTI

Fish and Cottage Cheese Curry

Serves 4

Fish that may be used are pomfret, rawas and surmai.

750 gm fish steaks, cleaned.

For marinade:

½ tsp turmeric powder
2 tbsp lime juice
½ tsp salt

1 tbsp plain flour
1 tbsp oil
½ tsp black mustard seeds
3 large dried red chillies, deseeded and chopped
½ tsp cumin powder
½ tsp coriander powder
½ tsp turmeric powder
1 tsp sugar
500 gm cottage cheese, cubed
Salt to taste
1 tbsp chopped coriander leaves, to garnish

- Mix ingredients for marinade and rub into fish steaks. Keep for 15 minutes.

- Mix flour with water until it forms a thick smooth batter.

- Place flat-bottomed pan on medium heat and add oil. When oil is hot, add mustard seeds and chillies.

When mustard seeds start to splutter, take pan off fire and slowly add 2 cups water. Add all powdered spices and sugar. Place pan on low heat and let gravy simmer.

- Add fish steaks. Cover and cook for 10 minutes.

- Add cottage cheese and batter and stir gently. Cook for 5 minutes till gravy is very thick.

- Garnish with chopped coriander and serve hot with bhakris.

BORATLI MACHHI

Fish Curry with Bora

Serves 4

Fish that may be used are pomfret, rawas and surmai.

750 gm fish steaks, cleaned.

For *marinade*:

½ tsp turmeric powder
2 tbsp lime juice
½ tsp salt

2 tbsp oil
4 green chillies, slit longitudinally
1 large onion, chopped
1 tsp sugar
1 tsp ginger paste
1 tsp garlic paste
½ tsp cumin powder
½ tsp coriander powder
½ tsp chilli powder
500 gm large ripe bora, deseeded and halved
½ tsp garam masala powder
Salt to taste

- Mix ingredients for marinade and rub into fish steaks. Keep for 15 minutes.
- Place flat-bottomed pan on medium heat and add oil. When oil is hot, add chillies and fry for 1 minute. Add onion and fry till brown.

- Add sugar, ginger, garlic, and all spices except garam masala and fry for 1 minute.

- Add 1 cup water, boras and fish steaks. Cover and cook for 10 minutes adding water as required. When fish is cooked, add garam masala, cover and turn off heat.

- Serve hot with freshly steamed rice.

BAGDACHEY KALWAN

Fish-Head Tamarind Curry

Serves 4

This is made from leftover fish-heads. Fish-heads can also be bought from fish vendors at a very reasonable price.

4 large fish-heads, each cut into half, or 16 small fish-heads, cleaned and prepared.

- All other ingredients and method of cooking same as for Chinchecha Kalwan (Tamarind-Base Curry, see pp. 9-10).
- Serve hot with steamed rice.

NISTE KODI

Goa Fish Curry

Serves 4

This is the typical red fish curry from Goa. Any fish may be used.

750 gm fish steaks, cleaned. If using shrimps or prawns, shell, clean and leave whole.

½ tsp turmeric powder
6 cloves garlic, peeled
6 large dried red chillies, deseeded
1 large onion, chopped
2 tsp coriander seeds
1 pinch mace or nutmeg powder
2 tbsp freshly grated or desiccated coconut
1 tbsp tamarind purée
1 tbsp oil
Salt to taste

- Rub turmeric and a little salt into fish and marinate for 15 minutes.

- Grind all ingredients, except fish and oil, with a little water in an electric mixer or with a hand grinder to a thick chutney consistency. Set masala aside in bowl.

- Place flat-bottomed pan on medium heat and add oil. Before oil starts to smoke, add masala and fry lightly, ensuring that it retains its red colour and the coconut does not burn and turn brown. Add 2 cups water, bring to boil and lower heat.

- Add marinated fish along with marinade, 1 cup water and salt. Lower heat and cook for 10 minutes or until fish is done.

- Serve with freshly steamed rice.

KANE KADHI

Lady Fish Curry

Serves 4-6

This is a typical South Indian dish. Lady fish is a long lean fish about 6" to 9". It breeds only in brackish water where the sweet river water mingles with the salty water of the sea. This gives it an unusual flavour.

12 whole lady fish, cleaned.

½ tsp turmeric powder
1 tsp cumin seeds
1 tsp coriander seeds
1 large onion, chopped
6 cloves garlic, chopped
6 large dried red chillies
4 tbsp freshly grated or desiccated coconut
1 tbsp oil
8 curry leaves
Salt to taste

- Rub turmeric and a little salt into fish and marinate for 15 minutes.

- Grind all ingredients, except curry leaves and oil, with a little water in an electric mixer or with a hand grinder to thick chutney consistency.

- Place flat-bottomed pan on medium heat and add oil. Add ground masala and fry lightly. Add 2 cups water. Bring to a boil and lower heat.

- Add marinated fish along with marinade, curry leaves, 2 cups water and salt. Cover and cook for 10 minutes or until fish is done.

- Serve with freshly steamed rice.

MEENU THALA KADHI

Fish-Head Curry

Serves 2

(Recipe courtesy Rita Karnani)

This is a speciality of Kerala. This recipe has been exported
to the Far East, mainly to Malaysia and Singapore, by
Keralites living there, where a blend of Indian spices and
local ingredients like lemon grass make an unusual but
delicious dish. The fish-heads should be of medium size,
such as those of red snapper, rawas, surmai, seer fish or
king fish.

1 medium-sized fish-head, cleaned and prepared.

1 tsp turmeric powder
2 tbsp oil
1 tsp cumin powder
1 tsp coriander powder
1 tsp chilli powder
2 tomatoes, peeled (see p. 10) and chopped
5 green chillies, deseeded and halved
1 tbsp grated ginger
1 tbsp tamarind purée
6 cups coconut milk of medium consistency
10 okra, halved
4 aubergines, quartered
4 cherry tomatoes
Salt to taste

34

- Rub fish-head with turmeric and a little salt and marinate for 15 minutes.

- Heat oil on medium heat in wok. Add powdered spices and fry for ½ minute. Add tomatoes, chillies, ginger and tamarind and fry. Cover wok and cook for 5 minutes.

- Add half coconut milk and bring to boil on medium heat. Add marinated fish-head, okra and aubergines. Cover and cook until almost done. Add rest of coconut milk and cherry tomatoes. Cook till done.

- Serve piping hot in large bowl with steamed rice and iced sweet nimbu pani.

DAHI MACHH

Fish in Curd Curry

Serves 4

(Recipe courtesy Sangeeta Sengupta)

Fish that may be used in this traditional Bengali curry are rawas, surmai and bhetki.

750 gm fish steaks, cleaned, deboned and skinned.

3 tbsp mustard oil
4 green chillies
1 tsp yellow mustard seeds
1 tsp turmeric
500 gm curd
Salt to taste

- Heat 2 tbsp oil in wok. Before oil starts to smoke, add chunks of fish and deep-fry. Remove and set aside.

- Grind chillies, mustard seed and turmeric. Add curd to mixture and beat well. Add 1 tbsp oil and mix. Gently put in fried fish chunks.

- Place flat-bottomed pan on low fire and add fish mixture. Cover and cook on very low heat for 20 minutes.

- Serve with freshly steamed rice.

MACHHER KALIA

Fish Curry

Serves 4

(Recipe courtesy Sangeeta Sengupta)

Fish that may be used in this Bengali recipe are rawas, surmai and bhetki.

750 gm fish steaks, cleaned.

1 tsp turmeric powder
5 tbsp mustard oil
3 onions, sliced in thin strips, to garnish
1 tsp ginger paste
1 tsp garlic paste
½ tsp chilli powder
4 green chillies, slit lengthwise
Salt to taste
4 sprigs chopped coriander leaves, to garnish

- Rub ½ tsp turmeric and salt into fish and marinate for 15 minutes.

- Place wok on medium fire and heat oil. Deep-fry marinated fish until light brown and set aside to cool.

- Fry onion strips till golden brown, drain and keep aside.

- Add ginger and garlic and stir lightly. Put in turmeric and chilli powders. Add fried fish and stir.

Cover and cook for 2 minutes. When cooked, put in chillies.

- Garnish with chopped coriander and onion strips. Serve with freshly steamed rice.

CHINGRI MACHHER MALAIKARI

Prawns in Coconut Gravy

Serves 4-6

(Recipe courtesy Sangeeta Sengupta)

This is a typical Bengali dish.

2 kg medium-sized prawns, cleaned, shelled and deveined.

4 tbsp mustard oil
3 onions, finely sliced, to garnish
1 tsp turmeric powder
1½ tsp coriander powder
1½ tsp cumin powder
1½ tsp chilli powder
1 tsp sugar
1½ cup coconut milk of thick consistency
Salt to taste

- Place wok on medium heat and add oil. When oil is hot, deep-fry onion strips and set aside.

- Add marinated prawns and fry for 1 minute. Add powdered spices and sugar and stir for 1 minute. Add coconut milk. Cover and cook for 10 minutes.

- Garnish with crisp fried onion and serve with freshly steamed rice.

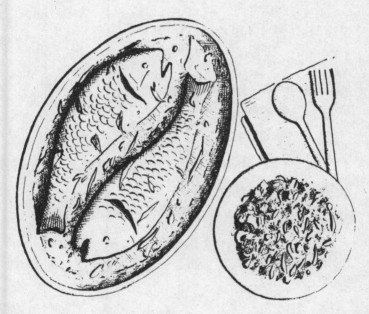

Stewed Fish in Chutney

KAIRICHYA CHATNITLI MACHHI

Raw Mango Chutney Fish

Serves 4

Fish that may be used are pomfret, surmai, rawas, pala, Bombay duck, whitebait, mandeli, shrimp, prawn and lobster.

750 gm fish steaks, cleaned. If using whitebait, mandeli or shellfish, clean and leave whole.

For marinade:

1 level tsp turmeric powder
1 tbsp lime juice
½ tsp salt

1 tbsp oil
1 cup green masala (see p. 3)
1 heaped tbsp peeled and minced raw mango
½ tsp sugar
¼ tsp garam masala powder
Salt to taste

- Mix ingredients for marinade, rub into fish and marinate for 15 minutes.

- Place flat-bottomed pan on medium heat and add oil. Before oil starts to smoke, add green masala and minced mango. Fry lightly, ensuring that green colour is retained and coconut does not burn and turn brown.

- Add marinated fish along with marinade and very little water to get a thick, almost dry consistency. Add sugar and salt. Cover and cook for 10 minutes or until fish is done.

- Add garam masala, turn off heat and keep covered for 2 minutes.

- Serve with rice, dal, and koshimbir.

TADITLI KALI MACHHI

Black Masala Chutney and Toddy Fish

Serves 4

Fish that may be used are pomfret, surmai, rawas, gol fish, pala, mandeli, karandi, jawla, shrimp, prawn, crab, lobster, oyster, clam, dried Bombay ducks halved, and dried shrimp.

750 gm fish steaks, cleaned. If using oysters, clean and take off the shell. If using clams and mussels, clean and leave on shell.

For marinade:

1 tsp turmeric powder
1 tsp lime juice
½ tsp salt

1 tbsp oil
1 cup coconut black masala (see p. 5)
1 tsp lime juice
½ tsp sugar
¼ tsp garam masala powder
1 tbsp toddy or coconut feni
Salt to taste

- Mix ingredients for marinade, rub into fish and marinate for 15 minutes.

- Heat oil in flat-bottomed pan on medium heat. Fry coconut black masala. Add marinated fish along with marinade, lime juice, sugar and salt. Add very little water to get thick, almost dry consistency.

Cover and cook for 10 minutes or until fish is done. Do not overcook shellfish or it will turn rubbery.

- Add garam masala, toddy or feni and turn off heat. Keep covered for 2 minutes.

- Serve with bhakri or freshly steamed rice and spring onion.

AMSULATLI LAL MACHHI

Red Chilli Chutney and Amsul Fish

Serves 4

Fish that may be used are pomfret, bangda, boi, shrimp, prawn, lobster, crab, oyster, clam, mussel, dried Bombay duck halved, and dried shrimp.

750 gm fish steaks, cleaned. If using shrimps, prawns, oysters, clams or mussels, shell, clean and leave whole.

For marinade:

1 tsp lime juice
1 level tsp turmeric powder
½ tsp salt

1 tbsp oil
1 cup coconut red chilli masala (see p. 4)
4 pods amsul, soaked in 1 tbsp water
1 tbsp lime juice
½ tsp sugar
Salt to taste

- Mix ingredients for marinade, rub into fish and marinate for 15 minutes.
- Place flat-bottomed pan on medium heat and add oil. Before oil starts to smoke, add coconut red masala and fry lightly, ensuring that bright red colour is retained and coconut does not burn and turn brown.

- Add marinated fish along with marinade, amsul along with water in which it was soaked, lime juice, sugar and salt. Add very little water to get thick, almost dry consistency. Cover and cook for 10 minutes or until fish is done.

- Serve with bhakri and spring onion.

KANDE BATATYATLI MACHHI

Onion Masala Fish

Serves 4

Fish that may be used are bangda, boi, whitebait, jawla, karandi, shrimp, prawn, lobster, oyster, mussel and clam, dried Bombay duck halved, and dried shrimp.

750 gm fish, cleaned. If using oysters, clean and remove shell. If using mussels or clams, shell may be retained or removed.

For marinade:

1 tsp turmeric powder
1 tsp lime juice
½ tsp chilli powder
1 tsp grated ginger
1 tsp minced garlic
½ tsp salt

1 tbsp oil
2 cloves
1" piece cinnamon
2 green chillies, slit lengthwise
¼ tsp cardamom powder
¼ tsp coriander powder
¼ tsp cumin powder
2 medium onions, sliced
1 large potato, peeled and cubed
1 tsp jaggery or sugar
1 large tomato, peeled (see p. 10) and chopped
1 pinch mace or nutmeg powder
1 tbsp coconut feni or toddy
Salt to taste
1 tbsp coriander leaves, to garnish

Stewed Fish in Chutney   **49**

- Mix ingredients for marinade, rub into fish and marinate for 15 minutes.

- Place large frying pan on medium heat and add oil. Before oil starts to smoke, add whole cloves and cinnamon. When spices start to splutter, add green chillies, powdered spices and fry for ½ minute.

- Add onion and fry until translucent. Put in potatoes, jaggery or sugar, salt and 1 cup water. Cover and cook over low heat.

- When potatoes are nearly cooked, add marinated fish along with marinade, tomato and ½ cup water. Cover and cook for 10 minutes until fish is done and gravy is thick. Add mace or nutmeg powder and turn off heat. Pour in toddy or coconut feni. Cover for 2 minutes.

- Garnish with chopped coriander. Serve with bhakri or freshly steamed rice. Leftovers make a tasty filling for sandwiches.

CHINCHA GULATLA JAWLA

Sweet and Sour Prawn

Serves 4-6

8 cups very small prawns, cleaned.

½ tsp turmeric powder
1 tbsp oil
2 medium onions, chopped
1 tbsp grated ginger
1 tbsp minced garlic
1 tsp coriander powder
1 tsp cumin powder
1 tsp chilli powder
4 tbsp crumbled jaggery or 4 tsp sugar
4 tbsp tamarind purée
Salt to taste
2 tbsp chopped coriander leaves, to garnish

- Rub turmeric and ¼ tsp salt into fish. Marinate for 15 minutes.

- Place flat-bottomed pan on medium heat and add oil. Add onion, ginger, garlic and powdered spices. Fry till onion is dark brown.

- Add jaggery, tamarind, 1 tsp salt and 1½ cups water. Mix well and cook for 5 minutes. Add marinated prawns along with marinade and ½ cup water. Cover and cook on low heat for 10 minutes or more until almost dry.

- Garnish with chopped coriander. Serve with spring onions and bhakri. Leftovers make a tasty filling for sandwiches.

CHATNI ANI KELYATLA SARANGA

Pomfret with Green Masala Chutney and Bananas

Serves 4

750 gm pomfret steaks, cleaned.

For marinade:

½ tsp turmeric powder
1 tsp lime juice
½ tsp salt

1 large ripe banana, peeled
1 tbsp oil
1 cup green masala (see p. 3)
Salt to taste

- Mix ingredients for marinade, rub into fish and marinate for 15 minutes.

- Halve banana, lengthwise. Halve each piece across, making four pieces in all.

- Place flat-bottomed pan on medium heat and add oil. Before oil starts to smoke, add banana and fry lightly till golden brown.

- Add green masala and fry for 2 minutes. Add marinated fish along with marinade, 2 cups water and cover. Lower heat and cook for 10 minutes till fish is done. Ensure a thick consistency.

- Serve with chapati or freshly steamed rice.

Stewed Fish in Chutney

DAHYATLEY SUKKA

Dried Fish with Curd

Serves 4

12 dried Bombay duck, cleaned and prepared, and cut into 4 pieces
each.

For marinade:

¾ tsp turmeric
3 tbsp lime juice
1 tsp cumin powder

2 tbsp oil
1 tbsp ginger paste
1 tbsp garlic paste
4 tbsp white sesame seeds, ground to paste with 2 tbsp water
4 green chillies, slit lengthwise
500 gm curd, beaten well
4 medium-sized boiled potatoes, sliced
Salt to taste

- Mix ingredients for marinade, rub into fish and marinate for 15 minutes.
- Place flat-bottomed pan on medium heat. Add oil. When oil is hot, add ginger, garlic, sesame paste and green chillies. Fry for 1 minute.
- Add 2 cups water. Add fish pieces and cook for 1 minute. Lower heat, cover and cook for 10 minutes.
- Add curd and cook for 5 minutes. Add potatoes and stir gently and cook without lid for 2 minutes. It will

be of stew consistency. Put off heat, cover and leave for 2 minutes.

- Serve hot with bhakri.

MUGATLI MACHHI

Fish Stew with Sprouts

Serves 4

Fish that may be used are pomfret, rawas and surmai.

750 gm fish steaks, cleaned.

For marinade:

1 tsp turmeric
2 tbsp lime juice
½ tsp salt

2 tbsp oil
6 curry leaves
1 cup green masala (see p. 3)
½ tsp chilli powder
½ tsp cumin powder
½ tsp coriander powder
500 gm green moong sprouts
Salt to taste

- Mix ingredients for marinade, rub into fish and leave for 15 minutes.
- Place flat-bottomed pan on medium heat and add oil. When oil is hot, add curry leaves. When they start to splutter, add all remaining ingredients, except fish.
- Add 1 cup water, cover and cook on low heat for 10 minutes or till sprouts are almost done.

- Add fish steaks along with the marinade, add 1 cup water or as necessary, cover and cook for 10 minutes.

- Serve stew with steamed rice and koshimbir.

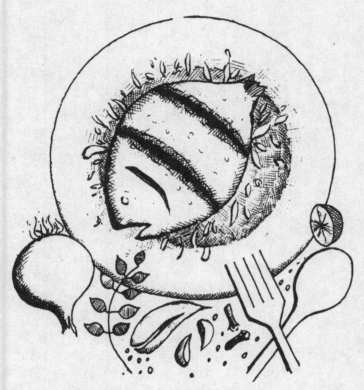

Pan-Fried Fish

KOTHMIRIT TALLELI MACHHI

Coriander Fried Fish

Serves 4

This is a good accompaniment to aperitifs. Fish that may be used are pomfret, gol fish, surmai, rawas, pala, Bombay duck, bangda, boi, whitebait, mandeli, prawn, lobster, shelled mussel, clam and oyster.

1 kg fish steaks, cleaned. If using boi, whitebait and mandeli, clean and leave whole.

For marinade:

½ tsp turmeric powder
1 tsp lime juice
1 tsp sugar
½ tsp salt

For masala:

2 bunches coriander leaves, chopped
2 green chillies, chopped
1" piece ginger, peeled and chopped
8 cloves garlic, peeled and chopped

Oil, for frying
1 cup rice flour (optional)
Salt to taste
Lime wedges, to garnish

- Mix ingredients for marinade and rub into fish. Marinate for 15 minutes.

- Grind all ingredients for masala with very little water with an electric mixer or a hand grinder into a smooth paste. Rub paste into fish and leave for 15 minutes.

- If using rice flour, spread evenly on large plate and, ensuring that each piece of fish is well covered with the green masala, press each side gently on the layer of flour.

- Over medium heat, put oil in frying pan for shallow-frying or in wok for deep-frying.

- Fry fish for not more than 10 minutes. Take care to turn the fish over if shallow-frying. The fish can also be barbecued.

- Garnish with lime wedges.

LAL MASALYATLI TALLELI MACHHI

Red Chilli Fried Fish

Serves 4

This makes a good accompaniment to aperitifs. Fish that may be used are pomfret, gol fish, surmai, rawas, pala, Bombay duck, bangda, boi, whitebait, mandeli, prawn, lobster, shelled mussel, clam and oyster.

1 kg fish steaks, cleaned. If using boi, whitebait and mandeli, clean and leave whole. If using Bombay duck, prepare and halve.

2 tsp chilli powder
2 tsp cumin powder
2 tsp coriander powder
1 tsp turmeric powder
2 tbsp lime juice
2 cups rice flour (optional)
Oil, for frying
Salt to taste
Lime wedges, to garnish

- Mix all ingredients, except flour and oil, and rub into fish. Marinate for 15 minutes.

- If using rice flour, spread evenly on large plate and press each side of fish gently on the layer of flour, coating it evenly.

- Over medium heat, put oil in frying pan for shallow-frying or in wok for deep-frying.

- Fry fish for not more than 10 minutes. Take care to turn fish over if shallow-frying. The fish can also be barbecued.

- Garnish with lime wedges.

TIKHAT MASALYAT TALLELI MACHHI

Piquant Masala Fried Fish

Serves 4

Fish that may be used are pomfret, gol fish, surmai, rawas, pala, Bombay duck, bangda, boi, whitebait, mandeli, prawn, lobster, shelled mussel, clam, oyster and fish roe.

1 kg fish steaks, cleaned. If using boi, whitebait and mandeli, clean and leave whole. If using fish roe, steam for 10 minutes and slice in ¼" thick round slices.

For marinade:

1 tsp turmeric powder
2 tbsp lime juice
½ tsp salt

For masala:

2 bunches coriander leaves, chopped
2 green chillies, chopped
1" piece ginger, peeled and chopped
8 cloves garlic, peeled and chopped
2 tsp chilli powder
2 tsp cumin powder
2 tsp coriander powder

1 cup rice flour (optional)
Oil, for frying
Salt to taste
Lime wedges, to garnish

- Mix ingredients for marinade and rub into fish. Marinate for 15 minutes.

- Grind all ingredients for masala with very little water in an electric mixer or with a hand grinder to a smooth paste. Rub paste into fish and marinate for 15 minutes.

- Spread rice flour evenly on a large plate and press each side of fish gently on the layer of flour, coating it evenly.

- Over medium heat, put oil in frying pan for shallow-frying or in wok for deep-frying.

- Fry fish for not more than 10 minutes. Take care to turn fish over if shallow-frying.

- Garnish with lime wedges. Serve with whole spring onion, rice and dal.

MITH MIRYATLI MACHHI

Salt-and-Pepper Fish

Serves 4

Fish that may be used are pomfret, gol fish, surmai, rawas, pala and bangda. The fish can either be fried or baked.

1 kg fish steaks, cleaned.

1 tbsp roughly ground black pepper
1 tsp finely ground black pepper
2 tbsp lime juice
Salt to taste
Lime wedges, to garnish

For baking:

2 tbsp butter or ghee
Sprigs of coriander leaves
Banana leaf, softened by holding over low fire and cut into pieces, or baking foil

- Rub salt, pepper and lime juice into fish and marinate for 15 minutes.

For frying:

- Heat butter or ghee over medium heat in frying pan. Shallow-fry fish for 10 minutes. Turn fish over while frying.

For baking:

- Individually wrap marinated fish steaks with a sprig of fresh coriander leaves, in pieces of banana leaf or baking foil and secure with a toothpick.

- Bake in baking dish in pre-heated oven at 180°C (350°F) for 20 minutes.

- Serve with lime wedges.

AMBAT DAHYATLI MACHHI

Fried Sour Cream Fish

Serves 4

This can be served as a hors d'ouvre. Fish that may be used are pomfret, rawas and surmai.

1 kg fish steaks, cleaned.

2 cups sour cream
4 tsp freshly ground pepper
1 tsp salt
1 tbsp ginger paste
1 tbsp garlic paste
6 cups breadcrumbs
Oil, for frying
Spring onions, to garnish

- Mix all ingredients except oil, breadcrumbs and fish. Rub mixture well onto each fish steak. Refrigerate for 30 minutes.

- Spread breadcrumbs onto flat plate. Cover each fish steak with breadcrumbs on both sides.

- Place round-bottomed frying pan for deep-frying on high heat. Add sufficient oil. When oil starts to smoke, lower heat to medium and deep-fry breaded fish steaks till golden brown.

- Serve garnished with slivers of fresh spring onions.

TALLELI GABOLI

Fried Masala Fish Roe

Serves 4

1 kg large fish roe, cleaned and steamed for 30 minutes, skin
removed and cut into ½" rounds.

For dry masala:

1 tsp turmeric powder
2 tsp chilli powder
2 tsp cumin powder
2 tsp coriander powder
1 tsp garam masala powder
1 tsp salt

For green masala:

4 green chillies, deseeded and chopped
1" piece ginger, peeled and chopped
6 cloves garlic, peeled and chopped
3 bunches coriander leaves, chopped
1 tsp sugar
1 tsp salt
2 tbsp lime juice

Oil, for frying

- Mix ingredients for dry masala and rub on each slice
  of roe and let them stand for 5 minutes.

- Mix ingredients for green masala and grind in an
  electric mixer or with a hand grinder. Rub on top of
  dry masala on each slice and keep for 5 minutes.

- Place large shallow frying pan on high heat. Add enough oil and heat until it smokes.

- Add 1 or 2 slices of roe at a time, giving enough space to turn it over without breaking. Fry on high heat until brown on both sides.

- Serve hot as hors d'oeuvre or with bhakri and fresh spring onions.

TARELA MASALA BOOMLA

Fried Spiced Lamprey

Serves 4

(Recipe courtesy Bhicoo Manekshaw)

This is a typical Parsi dish.

12 fresh boomla, cleaned.

½ tsp fenugreek powder
1 tsp cumin powder

For masala:

4 green chillies, deseeded
2" piece ginger, peeled and chopped
6 cloves garlic, peeled and chopped
1 tsp turmeric powder
5 dried red chillies, deseeded
1 tsp cumin powder
2 tsp coriander powder
1 tsp fenugreek seeds
1 large stick cinnamon, broken into bits
2-3 cloves
3 white cardamoms
4 black peppercorns

Juice of 2 limes
Rice flour, as required
Sesame seed oil, for frying
Salt to taste
Lime wedges, to garnish

- Remove head, fins and bones jutting out above tail from fish. Remove insides without tearing soft skin.

- Mix fenugreek and cumin powders and rub into fish.

- Grind all ingredients for masala with a little water in an electric mixer or with a hand grinder. Add lime juice to masala, rub well over fish and leave for 30 minutes.

- Roll each fish in rice flour, and cover well.

- Heat oil on hot griddle. Add boomla and lower heat. Fry till side is crisp. Turn over and fry other side.

- Serve hot with lime wedges and rotis.

TALLELI BANGDE

Fried Fresh Mackerel

Serves 4

This is a popular Goan dish.

12 medium-sized whole mackerels, cleaned.

8 large dried red chillies
2 tsp cumin seeds
2 tsp coriander seeds
1 tsp turmeric powder
2 tbsp tamarind purée
Oil, for deep-frying
Salt to taste
Lime wedges, to garnish

- Grind all ingredients, except fish and oil, to a fine paste in an electric mixer or with a hand grinder. Rub masala into fish and marinate for 30 minutes.

- Heat oil in wok on medium heat for deep-frying. When oil is very hot, deep-fry marinated fish individually till crisp.

- Serve with lime wedges.

Pulaos

SARANGYACHA PULAO

Pomfret Pulao

Serves 4

This is best with pomfret though other fish such as rawas or surmai may be used.

1 kg fish steaks, cleaned.

For marinade:

1 tsp turmeric powder
2 tsp lime juice
½ tsp salt

For masala:

6 large dried red chillies, deseeded and chopped
1" piece ginger, roughly diced
8 cloves garlic, peeled
3 tbsp fresh or desiccated coconut
1" piece cinnamon, broken into bits
2 cloves
½ tsp cardamom powder
½ tsp coriander powder
½ cumin powder
1 aniseed powder
1 pinch mace or nutmeg powder
1 tsp salt

2 tbsp oil
1 large onion, chopped
1 bay leaf
2 cups long-grained rice, washed
1 tsp salt

1 tbsp chopped coriander leaves, to garnish
1 tbsp freshly ground coconut, to garnish

- Mix ingredients for marinade, rub into fish and marinate for 15 minutes.

- Grind all ingredients for masala with little water with an electric mixer or a hand grinder into a smooth paste.

- Place flat-bottomed pan on medium heat and add 1 tbsp oil. Before oil starts to smoke, add onion and fry till transparent. Add ground masala and fry for 3 minutes. Retain chutney consistency.

- Add marinated fish along with marinade. Add ½ cup water. Cover and allow to cook on low heat for 5 minutes. Keep aside.

- Place large flat-bottomed pan on medium heat. Add 1 tbsp oil. Before oil starts to smoke, add bay leaf.

- When bay leaf starts to splutter, turn heat to minimum and add rice. Fry for 2 minutes and put off heat. Add ½ tsp salt and cover rice with water, twice the level of rice.

- Over low heat, cover and cook for 15 minutes, checking periodically whether extra water is required. When rice grains are fairly firm and separate and can be crushed easily with thumb and forefinger, it is cooked. Turn off heat and set aside.

- Remove half the quantity of rice into a bowl. Pour half the fish over rice remaining in pan. Cover with rice in bowl. Pour rest of the fish evenly on top.

- Cover pan tightly and cook on low heat for 5 minutes. Turn off heat but keep tightly covered for another 5 minutes.

- Garnish with coconut and chopped coriander. Serve with koshimbir.

PATICHA ANI KOLAMBICHA PULAO

Prawn Lemon Grass Pulao

Serves 4

This pulao has a pale yellow colour and a delicate fragrance of lemon grass.

> 2 cups prawns or shrimps, cleaned and prepared.

For marinade:

> ½ tsp turmeric powder
> 1 tsp lime juice
> ½ tsp salt

> 2 tbsp butter or ghee
> 1 large onion, chopped
> 1 tbsp freshly ground black pepper
> 1 tsp minced garlic
> 12 strips lemon grass, each 4" long, fresh or dried, cleaned
> 2 cups long-grained rice, washed
> 1 tsp salt
> 1 tbsp chopped coriander leaves, to garnish

- Mix ingredients for marinade, rub into fish and marinate for 15 minutes.
- Place flat-bottomed pan on medium heat and add butter or ghee. As soon as butter or ghee melts, add onion, pepper, garlic and lemon grass. Fry until onion is transparent.

- Add marinated prawns along with marinade. Put on low heat cover and cook for 3 minutes. Add rice, 1 tsp salt and cover rice with water, twice the level of rice.

- Cover and cook for 15 minutes, checking occasionally whether extra water is required. When rice grains are fairly firm and separate and can be crushed easily with thumb and forefinger, it is cooked.

- Remove strips of lemon grass. Garnish with chopped coriander. Serve with koshimbir.

SHIMPLYA ANI TOMATOCHA PULAO

Shellfish and Tomato Piquant Pulao

Serves 4

Fish that may be used are prawn, shrimp, jawla, karandi, oyster, clam and mussel.

2 cups shellfish, cleaned, shelled and prepared.

For marinade:

1 tsp turmeric powder
1 tsp lime juice
½ tsp salt

1 medium onion, chopped
1 bay leaf
6 whole peppercorns
6 whole cardamoms
2" piece cinnamon
4 cloves
2 large tomatoes, peeled (see p. 10) and diced
1 tsp grated ginger
1 tsp minced garlic
1 tsp chilli powder
1 pinch mace or nutmeg powder
1tsp garam masala powder
2 tsp sugar
200 gms cashewnuts
2 cups long-grained rice, washed
2 tbsp oil
1 tsp salt
1 tbsp chopped coriander leaves, to garnish

Spring onions, to garnish
1 grilled baby tomato, to garnish

- Mix ingredients for marinade, rub into fish and marinate for 15 minutes.

- Place flat-bottomed pan on medium heat and add oil. Before oil starts to smoke, add bay leaf, peppercorns, cardamom, cinnamon, cloves and fry for 2 minutes. Add onion and fry till transparent.

- Add tomatoes, ginger, garlic, powdered spices, sugar and cashewnuts. Fry for 3 minutes.

- Add marinated shellfish along with marinade and 1 cup water. Cover and cook for 3 minutes on low heat.

- Add rice to fish and mix thoroughly. Cover rice with water, twice the level of rice.

- Cover and cook on low heat for 15 minutes, checking periodically whether extra water is required. When rice grains are fairly firm and separate and can be crushed easily with thumb and forefinger, it is cooked.

- Remove the bay leaf, peppercorns, cardamom, cinnamon and cloves. Garnish with chopped coriander and spring onions. A whole grilled baby tomato may be placed on top in the center of the pulao.

SODEY WANGYACHA PULAO

Prawn Pulao with Baby Aubergines

Serves 4

2 cups fresh or dried prawns, cleaned and prepared. If using dried
prawns, soak in cold water for 10 minutes.

For marinade:

1 tsp turmeric powder
1 tsp lime juice
½ tsp salt

2 tbsp oil
2 large onions, chopped
3 tbsp desiccated coconut
2 green chilli, chopped
1 tsp grated ginger
1 tsp minced garlic
1 tsp freshly ground black pepper
½ tsp cardamom powder
1 tsp coriander powder
1 tsp cumin powder
½ tsp chilli powder
½ tsp garam masala powder
1 tsp sugar
8 baby aubergines, quartered halfway from the top
8 baby potatoes, peeled
2 cups long-grained rice, washed
Salt to taste
1 tbsp chopped coriander leaves, to garnish
Lime wedges, to garnish

- Mix ingredients for marinade, rub into fish and marinate for 15 minutes.

- Place flat-bottomed pan on medium heat and add oil. Before oil starts to smoke, add onion and fry till transparent. Add coconut and fry for 1 minute till it starts to brown. Add chilli, ginger, garlic, powdered spices and sugar. Fry for 1 minute.

- Add aubergines, potatoes and 1 cup water. Cover and cook for 10 minutes on low heat.

- Add marinated prawns along with marinade. Add rice and 1 tsp salt to prawns and vegetables and mix thoroughly. Cover rice with water, twice the level of rice.

- Cover and cook on low heat for 15 minutes, checking periodically whether extra water is required. When rice grains are fairly firm and separate and can be crushed easily with thumb and forefinger, it is cooked.

- Garnish with fresh coriander and lime wedges.

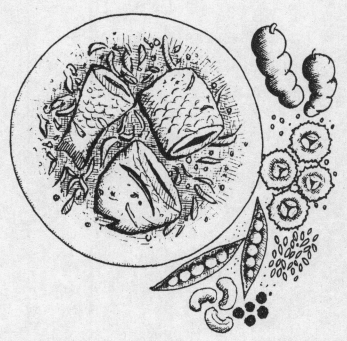

Speciality Seafood

BHAJLELA SARANGA

Baked Fish

Serves 4

This entrée makes a good piéce de rèsistance at parties. Fish that may be used are pomfret, surmai or rawas.

2 kg whole pomfret or surmai or rawas, cleaned and prepared.

For marinade:

1 tsp turmeric powder for pomfret
(1 tbsp turmeric powder for surmai or rawas)
1 tbsp lime juice
½ tsp salt

1 cup green masala, fairly dry (see p. 3)
Salt to taste
Chopped coriander leaves, to garnish
Lime wedges, to garnish
Tomato slices, to garnish
Spring onions, to garnish

Banana leaf, softened over low flame, or baking foil
1 tsp oil, to grease baking tray and banana leaf or baking foil

- Place fish on a non-slip chopping board. With a sharp knife, make horizontal superficial cuts piercing skin and only part of flesh. Cuts should be made at equal distances as when slicing fish steaks.

- Mix ingredients for marinade and rub over fish and inside cuts. Marinate for 15 minutes.

- Pre-heat oven at 180°C (350°F). Grease large baking tray. Lay out large banana leaf or baking foil and place the whole fish on it.

- Coat fish with green masala to about ⅛" thickness. Gently but quickly turn over and coat other side. Wrap banana leaf or baking foil around fish and secure with wooden toothpicks.

- Bake for 30 minutes. It is necessary to check if the surmai or rawas is properly cooked as its thickness varies. Remove wrapping carefully without breaking fish.

- Serve garnished with spring onions, lime wedges and tomato slices. Sprinkle fish with chopped coriander.

- Individual fish steaks may also be prepared in this way.

KAJUNI BHARLELA SARANGA

Stuffed Pomfret with Cashewnuts

Serves 4-6

The fish can either be baked or fried.

1 kg whole pomfret, cleaned and prepared for stuffing.

For marinade:

1 tsp turmeric powder
½ tsp salt
1 tbsp lime juice

For stuffing:

3 tbsp oil
1" piece cinnamon
2 cloves
12 seedless sultanas
12 cashewnuts
¼ tsp cardamom powder
¼ tsp coriander powder
¼ tsp cumin powder
½ tsp aniseed powder
½ tsp turmeric powder
1 pinch mace or nutmeg powder
1 medium onion, chopped
1 tsp sugar
1 cup green masala (see p. 3)
1 tbsp lime juice
Salt to taste

1 tbsp chopped coriander leaves, to garnish
Lime wedges, to garnish

Spring onions, to garnish

Banana leaf, softened by holding over low flame, or baking foil
1 tsp oil, to grease baking tray

- Place flat-bottomed pan on medium heat and add 1 tbsp oil. Before oil starts to smoke, add cinnamon and cloves. When spices starts to splutter, add sultanas, cashewnuts and powdered spices. Fry for 1 minute. Add onion and sugar. Fry till onion turns golden brown. Add green masala and 1 tbsp lime juice.

- Cook on low heat for 5 minutes, stirring constantly, until green masala is dry. Ensure that it retains its green colour and does not turn brown.

- Remove cinnamon and cloves. Remove stuffing from fire and cool to room temperature.

- Rub a little oil on either side of fish. With one hand, gently lift cut flap of fish and, with other hand, fill right through with stuffing. Carefully turn fish over and stuff other side. Take care not to over-stuff fish as it will ruin its shape.

- Tie twine around the fish to keep the stuffing in place. Any extra stuffing may be served on the side.

For baking:

- Grease baking tray and lay banana leaf or foil on it.

- Wrap banana leaf or foil around fish and secure with wooden toothpicks.

92

- Bake at 180° (350°F) for 30 minutes.
- When fish is cooked, remove wrapping and discard.

For frying:

- If frying the fish, use a large non-stick frying pan and sufficient oil as the skin of the pomfret is very delicate and will break easily. A large pan will help when turning fish.

- Cut away twine with a pair of scissors and remove carefully.
- Garnish with lime wedges, spring onions and chopped coriander.

Pomfret can also be stuffed with coconut red chilli masala (see p. 4). Fry masala with onion, sultanas, cashewnuts, lime juice and sugar.

KANDEY LASUNACHA SARANGA

Pomfret with Onion and Garlic Stuffing

Serves 4-6

The fish can either be baked or fried.

2 kg whole pomfret, cleaned and prepared for stuffing.

For marinade:

2 tsp turmeric powder
2 tbsp lime juice
1 tsp salt

For stuffing:

3 tbsp oil
2 medium onions, chopped
2 cups groundnuts, roughly pounded and roasted
2 tsp grated ginger
2 tsp minced garlic
½ tsp cardamom powder
½ tsp coriander powder
1 tsp cumin powder
1 tsp aniseed powder
1 tsp chilli powder
½ tsp turmeric powder
2 tsp sugar
2 tbsp lime juice
2 medium tomatoes, peeled (see p. 10) and diced
1 tsp garam masala powder
3 tbsp toddy or coconut feni
Salt to taste

2 tbsp chopped coriander leaves, to garnish
Lime wedges, to garnish

Spring onions, to garnish

Banana leaf, softened by holding over low flame, or baking foil
1 tsp oil, to grease baking tray

- Place flat-bottomed pan on medium heat and add 1 tbsp oil. Before oil starts to smoke, add onion and fry till golden brown. Add groundnuts and fry for 2 minutes. Add ginger, garlic, powdered spices except garam masala, sugar and lime juice, and fry for 3 minutes.

- Add tomatoes and garam masala, and cook for 10 minutes or until almost dry. Turn off heat, add toddy and cover. Allow to cool at room temperature.

- Rub a little oil on either side of fish. With one hand, gently lift cut flap of fish and with other hand, fill right through with stuffing. Take care not to over-stuff fish as it will ruin its shape. Carefully turn fish over and stuff other side.

- Tie twine around fish to keep stuffing in place. Any extra stuffing may be served on the side.

For baking:

- Grease baking tray and lay banana leaf or baking foil on it. Place marinated pomfret on leaf or foil.

- Wrap banana leaf or foil around fish and secure with toothpicks.

- Bake at 180° (350°F) for 30 minutes.

- When fish is cooked, remove wrapping and discard.

For frying:

- Use large non-stick frying pan and sufficient oil as skin of pomfret is very delicate and fish may break easily. A large pan also helps in turning fish over.

- Cut away twine with a pair of scissors and remove carefully.

- Garnish with lime wedges, spring onions and chopped coriander.

KOLAMBINI BHARLELA SARANGA

Stuffed Pomfret with Prawns

Serves 4-6

The fish can either be baked or fried.

2 kg whole pomfret, cleaned and prepared.
2 cups small prawns, cleaned, shelled and marinated in ½ tsp
turmeric powder, ¼ tsp salt and 1 tsp lime juice for 15 minutes.

For marinade:

2 tsp turmeric
2 tbsp lime juice
½ tsp salt

For stuffing:

4 tbsp oil
2 medium onions, chopped
2 medium tomatoes, peeled (see p. 10) and diced
1 tsp grated ginger
2 tsp minced garlic
½ tsp cardamom powder
½ tsp coriander powder
1 tsp cumin powder
½ tsp aniseed powder
1 tsp chilli powder
½ tsp turmeric powder
2 tsp sugar
1 tbsp lime juice
½ tsp garam masala powder
3 tbsp toddy or coconut feni
Salt to taste

2 tbsp chopped coriander leaves, to garnish
Lime wedges, to garnish
Spring onions, to garnish

Banana leaf, softened by holding over low flame, or baking foil
1 tsp oil, to grease baking tray

- Mix ingredients for marinade, rub into pomfret and marinate for 15 minutes.

- Place flat-bottomed pan on medium heat and add 1 tbsp oil. Before oil starts to smoke, add onion and fry until golden brown. Add all other ingredients for stuffing, except garam masala and toddy, and fry for 5 minutes.

- Add prawns and garam masala and cook for 5 minutes until almost dry. Turn off heat, add toddy and cover. Allow to cool to room temperature.

- Rub a little oil on either side of fish. With one hand, gently lift cut flap of fish and with other hand, fill right through with stuffing. Take care not to overstuff fish as it will ruin its shape. Carefully turn fish over and stuff other side.

- Tie twine around fish to keep stuffing in place. Any extra stuffing may be served on the side.

For baking:

- Grease baking tray and lay banana leaf or baking foil on it. Place the marinated pomfret on leaf or foil.

- Wrap banana leaf or foil around fish and secure with wooden toothpicks.

- Bake at 180°C (350°F) for 30 minutes.
- When fish is cooked, remove wrapping and discard.

For frying:

- Use large non-stick frying pan and sufficient oil as skin of pomfret is very delicate and fish may break easily. A large pan also helps in turning fish over easily.

- Cut away twine with a pair of scissors and remove carefully.
- Garnish with lime wedges, spring onion, and chopped coriander.

KADHIPATYATLA SARANGA

Stuffed Pomfret with Curry Leaves Chutney

Serves 4-6

This preparation has an unusual flavour and aroma of curry leaves. The fish can either be baked or fried.

2 kg whole pomfret, cleaned and prepared.

For marinade:

2 tsp turmeric
2 tbsp lime juice
½ tsp salt

For stuffing:

1 bunch coriander leaves, chopped
8 sprigs curry leaves, separated from stalk and washed
4 green chillies, chopped
1" piece fresh ginger, peeled and chopped
12 cloves garlic, peeled
1 tsp coriander powder
1 tsp cumin powder
1 tsp aniseed powder
½ tsp turmeric powder
1 tsp garam masala powder
2 tsp sugar
1 tbsp lime juice

4 tbsp oil
2 medium onions, chopped
Salt to taste

Tomato slices, to garnish

Lime wedges, to garnish
Spring onions, to garnish

Banana leaf, softened by holding over low flame, or baking foil
1 tsp oil, to grease baking tray

- Combine all ingredients for stuffing, except oil, and with very little water, grind in an electric mixer or with a hand grinder. Set aside in bowl.

- Place flat-bottomed pan on medium heat and add 1 tbsp oil. Before oil starts to smoke, add onion and fry until golden brown. Add ground masala for stuffing and fry for 10 minutes until almost dry. Remove stuffing from fire and cool to room temperature.

- Rub a little oil on either side of fish. With one hand, gently lift cut flap of fish and with other hand, fill right through with stuffing. Carefully turn fish over and stuff other side.

For baking:

- Grease baking tray and lay banana leaf or baking foil on it. Place marinated pomfret on leaf or foil.

- Wrap banana leaf or foil around fish and secure with wooden toothpicks.

- Bake at 180°C (350°F) for 30 minutes.

- When fish is cooked, remove wrapping and discard.

For frying:

- Use a large non-stick frying pan and sufficient oil as skin of pomfret is very delicate and fish may break easily. A large pan also helps in turning fish over easily.

- Garnish with lime wedges, spring onion and tomato slices.

KOLAMBINI BHARLELI BHAJI

Stuffed Baked Vegetables with Prawns

Serves 4

Either fresh or dried prawns may be used.

2 cups fresh or dried small prawns, cleaned and prepared. If using
dried prawns, soak in cold water for 10 minutes.

For marinade:

1 tsp turmeric powder
1 tsp lime juice
1 tsp salt

8 medium capsicums or aubergines or tomatoes or 16 large okra
2 tbsp oil
1 large onion, finely chopped
1 tsp coriander powder
1 tsp cumin powder
1 tsp chilli powder
1 tsp grated ginger
1 tsp minced garlic
2 medium-sized tomatoes, peeled (see p. 10) and chopped
4 medium-sized potatoes, boiled and coarsely mashed
1 tsp sugar
½ tsp garam masala powder
2 tbsp chopped coriander leaves
1 tsp salt

- Mix ingredients for marinade, rub into fish and marinate for 15 minutes.

- Prepare vegetables for stuffing. Slice from top and save stem. If using tomato, with sharp knife remove pulp from tomato, chop pulp fine and keep aside. If using capsicum, discard inside and seeds. If using okra, make slit lengthwise in centre leaving intact ½" towards top and bottom. Remove and discard seeds and pulp.

- Wash vegetables in cold water and set aside.

For stuffing:

- Place flat-bottomed pan on medium heat and add 1 tbsp oil. Before oil starts to smoke add chopped onion and fry till transparent. Add powdered spices and 1 tsp salt and fry for 2 minutes.

- Add ginger, garlic, tomato, potato and sugar. Mix thoroughly, lower heat and cover. Cook for 10 minutes.

- Add prawns along with marinade and cook for 2 minutes.

- Remove from fire, add garam masala and chopped coriander, and mix. Allow stuffing to cool to room temperature.

- Rub remaining oil on outer skin of vegetables. Pack vegetables loosely with stuffing. Capsicum, aubergine and tomato may be closed on top with the sliced stem.

- Pre-heat oven to 180°C (350°F). Lightly grease baking dish and bake vegetables for 20 minutes. Aubergine may take longer depending on thickness of skin.

- Serve hot. For large setting, all four varieties of vegetables may be served.

BHAJI ANI KOLAMBICHA STEW

Stewed Vegetables with Prawns

Serves 4-6

The vegetables that may be used individually with prawns are chopped cabbage, cubed aubergines, cubed raw skinned jackfruit, cubed raw skinned papaya, cubed turnip, skinned baby potatoes, cauliflower florets and beans.

4 cups small or medium fresh or dried prawns, cleaned. If using dried prawns, soak in cold water for 10 minutes.

For marinade:

½ tsp turmeric powder
1 tsp lime juice
½ tsp salt

2 tbsp oil
2 medium onions, chopped
4 tbsp desiccated coconut
2 green chillies, chopped
1 tsp grated ginger
1 tsp minced garlic
½ tsp cardamom powder
1 tsp coriander powder
1 tsp cumin powder
1 tsp chilli powder
2 tsp sugar
6 cups vegetables, cut and cleaned
½ tsp garam masala powder
1 tsp salt

2 tbsp chopped coriander, to garnish

- Mix ingredients for marinade, rub into fish and marinate for 15 minutes.

- Place flat-bottomed pan on medium heat and add oil. Before oil starts to smoke, add onion and fry till transparent.

- Add coconut and fry for 1 minute making sure that it does not turn brown. Add chillies, ginger and garlic. Add powdered spices, sugar, 1 tsp salt and vegetables. Mix thoroughly and add 2 cups water. Cover and cook on low heat till vegetables are almost done.

- Add prawns along with marinade. Cover and cook for 5 minutes, till vegetables are almost dry. Remove from heat, add garam masala and cover for 2 minutes.

- Garnish with chopped coriander. Serve with bhakri.

AKHYA SHAHALYATLYA KOLAMBYA

Prawns in Whole Coconut

Serves 2

This is a good piéce de rèsistance for beach or garden parties.

10 large fresh prawns, cleaned and shelled.

1 medium green coconut

To fill coconut:

1 tbsp coconut feni or vodka
½ cup fresh cream
1 tsp freshly ground black pepper
¼ tsp salt
1 tbsp rice flour

Dill, to garnish

To prepare coconut:

- Slice off the top and keep.
- Empty coconut water into water jug. Do not disturb coconut flesh. Add coconut feni or vodka to coconut water in proportions of 1 part feni to 3 parts coconut water. Refrigerate.
- Slice off a bit on bottom of coconut so that it stands firmly on a flat surface.

- Rub in fresh cream, pepper, feni and salt into prawns and marinate for 20 minutes in refrigerator.

- Fill coconut with marinated prawns along with marinade.

- Make firm dough with rice flour, adding a little water. Close coconut with top slice. Seal edges all round with rice flour dough.

- Bake in open clay oven or in barbecue pit in the open, for 15 minutes. This is traditionally cooked in a bonfire. Check constantly to ensure that coconut does not burst. Do not cook this in closed kitchen oven as it may be extremely dangerous. Handle hot coconut with oven mittens and with a sharp knife pare off hard dough and prise open top.

- Ideally eat hot directly from the coconut with fruit forks but may be individually served in cocktail plates, garnished with dill. Add dash of fresh lime juice to refrigerated coconut water and feni cocktail. Serve in short cocktail glasses, laced with salt at the rim.

PALEBHAJITLI MACHHI

Greens with Pomfret

Serves 4

1 kg pomfret steaks, cleaned.

For marinade:

½ turmeric powder
½ tsp lime juice
½ tsp salt

1 bunch spinach
1 bunch fresh green dill
2 green chillies, chopped
8 cloves garlic, peeled
1 tbsp oil
1 tsp cumin powder
½ tsp gram masala powder
Salt to taste

- Mix ingredients for marinade, rub into fish and marinate for 15 minutes.

- Cut away stalks of spinach and dill, wash in salted water and drain. Adding some water, grind spinach, dill, green chillies and garlic together in an electric mixer or with a hand grinder, to chutney consistency. Set aside in a bowl.

- Place flat-bottomed pan on medium heat and add oil. Before oil starts to smoke, add cumin, salt and ground mixture. Fry lightly for 3 minutes. Cover and cook for 7 minutes on low heat.

- Add marinated fish along with marinade and 1 cup water. Cover and cook on low heat for 10 minutes until fish is cooked and gravy is thick. Turn off heat, add garam masala and keep covered for 2 minutes.

- Serve with freshly steamed rice and dal or with bhakri and spring onions.

RATYALATLI MACHHI

Fish Savoury with Sweet Potatoes

Serves 4

Fish that may be used are pomfret, rawas and surmai.

1 kg fish steaks, cleaned.

For marinade:

1 tsp grated ginger
1 tsp minced garlic
½ tsp salt

1 tbsp oil
6 black peppercorns
1" piece cinnamon
4 cloves
4 green chillies, slit lengthwise
4 medium sweet potatoes, peeled and cut into ½" rounds
2 cups coconut milk of medium consistency
¼ tsp mace or nutmeg powder
Salt to taste
1 tbsp chopped coriander leaves, to garnish

- Mix ingredients for marinade, rub into fish and marinate for 15 minutes.

- Place flat-bottomed pan on medium heat and add oil. Before oil starts to smoke, add peppercorns, cinnamon and cloves. When spices start to splutter, add chillies and sweet potato. Fry lightly for 3 minutes. Add ½ cup water, cover and cook for 5 minutes.

- Add marinated fish along with marinade, salt, and 1 cup water. Cover and cook for 10 minutes.

- Add coconut milk and cook for 2 minutes or until sweet potato and fish are done.

- Turn off heat, add mace or nutmeg powder and keep covered for 2 minutes.

- Carefully remove peppercorns, cinnamon and cloves and discard.

- Garnish with chopped coriander. Serve hot with steamed rice cakes.

KALA SARANGA

Black Pomfret

Serves 3-4

1 kg whole pomfret, cleaned.

For marinade:

½ tsp salt
2 tbsp lime juice

12 cloves, roasted and powdered
12 cardamoms, roasted and powdered
20 black peppercorns, roasted and powdered
5, 1" cinnamon sticks, roasted and powdered
1 tbsp cumin seeds, roasted and powdered
1 tbsp aniseed, roasted and powdered
4 tbsp tamarind purée
1 tsp sugar
Salt to taste

Banana leaf, softened by holding over low flame, or baking foil

- Make 6 horizontal cuts in flesh upto bone on either side of fish.
- Mix ingredients for marinade and rub into cuts. Marinate for 15 minutes.
- Mix remaining ingredients together into paste. Fill paste in cuts. Rub remaining paste all over.
- Wrap tightly with banana leaf or baking foil and secure with toothpicks.

- Bake at 180°C (350°F) for 30 minutes or till done.
- Unwrap carefully and serve with bhakris and spring onions.

AMSULATLI WAFLELI MACHHI

Baked Fish with Amsul

Serves 3-4

1 kg pomfret, rawas or surmai steaks, cleaned.

20 amsuls
2 tsp sugar
2 tsp fresh ground black pepper
1 tsp cumin powder
1 tsp coriander powder
½ tsp salt
½ tsp oil

Banana leaf, softened over low flame and cut into pieces, or baking foil

- Mix all ingredients, except fish and grind to thick paste in an electric mixer or with a hand grinder. Apply paste to each fish steak on both sides.

- Wrap individually with banana leaf or baking foil. Secure with toothpicks.

- Bake in oven at 180°C (350°F) for 30 minutes.

- Serve hot with bhakris.

SHEVANDI KANDA

King Prawn with Baby Onions

Serves 3-4

8 large king prawns, cleaned, shelled, with head and tail intact.

2 tbsp oil
8 curry leaves
1 large onion, finely chopped
1 tsp sugar
2 tbsp coconut vinegar
1½ tbsp freshly ground pepper
36 baby onions with skin removed
1½ cup coconut feni
Salt to taste

- Place large frying pan on medium heat and add oil. When oil is hot, add curry leaves and fry till crisp. Add chopped onion and fry till transparent. Add sugar, vinegar, pepper and salt. Fry for 1 minute.

- Prick baby onions with fork and add to pan. Fry for 3 minutes.

- Prick king prawns with fork and add to pan. Cover and cook on very low heat for 5 minutes.

- Add feni, cover and cook for 5 minutes or till prawns are done.

- Serve hot with freshly steamed rice.

TIKHAT MODKA

Spicy Whitebait

Serves 4-6

2 kg very small whitebait, cleaned.

2 tbsp oil
1 tsp whole cumin seeds
2 large bunches coriander leaves, ground with water to thick
consistency
1 tbsp garlic paste
4 green chillies, ground to paste
1 tsp sugar
2 tbsp lime juice
1 tsp garam masala powder
Salt to taste

- Place frying pan on medium heat and add oil. When oil is hot, add cumin seeds and fry till browned. Add coriander, garlic and chilli paste, sugar and salt and fry for 1 minute.

- Add whitebait, mix thoroughly, and add lime juice. Simmer, cover, lower heat and cook for 10 minutes. Add garam masala, turn off heat and keep covered for 2 minutes.

- Serve hot with rice cakes.

TADITLI KOLAMBI

Toddy Prawn

Serves 4

2 kg medium-sized prawns, cleaned and shelled.

1 tbsp oil
1 tbsp freshly ground black pepper
8 cloves garlic, skinned and lightly roasted
2 tsp ginger paste
8 ripe tomatoes, peeled (see p. 10) and chopped
2 tsp lime juice
2 cups coconut toddy
Salt to taste

- Place flat-bottomed pan on medium heat and add oil. When oil is hot, add pepper, garlic and ginger paste. Fry for 1 minute.

- Add tomatoes, salt and lime juice, stir and cook for 2 minutes.

- Add prawns and 1 cup toddy. Cover and cook for 5 minutes. Add remaining toddy, cover and cook for 5 more minutes. Turn off heat and keep for 2 minutes.

- Serve hot with bhakri or steamed rice. Green peppercorns preserved in vinegar may be served with this.

MAKUL ANI SAKHRET
BHAJLELEY KANDEY

Squid Masala with Caramelized Onions

Serves 4-6

1 kg squid, cleaned and cut in flat circles.

4 tbsp sugar
1 kg baby onions, skinned
2 tbsp oil
1½ cup coconut black masala (see p. 5)
2 tbsp coconut feni
¼ tsp nutmeg
Salt to taste

- Place frying pan on medium heat and spread sugar evenly in it. When it starts to caramelize and turn brown, prick onions with fork and add to pan.

- Coat onions well with caramel and add oil. Heat for 2 minutes and add coconut black masala and squid. Lower heat, cover and cook for 5 minutes till squid is done. Do not overcook, otherwise squid will turn rubbery.

- Add coconut feni and nutmeg. Turn off heat, cover and keep for 2 minutes.

- Serve hot with bhakri.

HIRVYA KELYATLA JAWLA

Prawn with Raw Bananas

Serves 4

1 kg tiny prawns, cleaned.

2 tbsp lime juice
1 tbsp ghee
1½ tbsp roughly ground black pepper
2 cups desiccated coconut
1 kg raw banana, cut in round slices
Salt to taste
1 cup chopped coriander leaves, to garnish

- Marinate prawns in lime juice for 15 minutes.
- Place frying pan on medium heat and add ghee. When ghee has melted, add pepper and coconut. Fry till coconut turns pale brown.
- Add banana slices with 1 cup water. Lower heat, cover and cook for 5 minutes.
- Add prawns along with marinade. Cover and cook for 10 minutes.
- Garnish with chopped coriander and serve with rice cakes.

PERUTLI CHIMBORI

Baked Crab in Guava

Serves 4

This can be served as a hor d'ouvres or as an entrée with large side salad.

4 tbsp crabmeat.

4 tbsp breadcrumbs
½ tsp chopped green chillies
¼ tsp ginger paste
¼ tsp garlic paste
1 tbsp chopped spring onion
1 tsp sour cream
1 tbsp lime juice
4 large ripe guavas
1 tsp oil
Salt to taste

- Add 2 tbsp breadcrumbs and all other ingredients, except guavas and oil, to crabmeat and mix thoroughly.

- Cut guavas into halves longitudinally and scoop out pulp and seeds. Prick inside lightly with fork. Brush outer skin with oil.

- Stuff guava shells with crab mixture and sprinkle remaining breadcrumbs on top.

- Grease baking dish and arrange stuffed guava shells in it.

- Bake in oven at 180°C (350°F) till guava shells are soft but firm.

KOLAMBICHA PITHALA

Prawn in Gram Flour

Serves 4

1 kg small prawns, cleaned and shelled.

2 tbsp oil
1 tsp mustard seeds
2 large onions, chopped
2 green chillies, chopped
1 tsp chilli powder
½ tsp turmeric powder
1 tsp sugar
1 cup gram flour
Salt to taste
Lime wedges, to garnish

- Place large frying pan on high heat and add oil. When the oil is hot, add mustard seeds, onion and chillies, and fry till golden brown. Add chilli powder, turmeric, sugar, salt and prawns. Fry for 10 minutes on medium heat.

- Add gram flour and stir-fry till mixture is completely dry.

- Garnish with lime wedges and serve hot with bhakris.

SHAHALYAT KALVEY

Oyster Green Masala with Fresh Coconut

Serves 4

1 kg large oysters, cleaned and prepared off the shell.

For marinade:

1 tsp turmeric powder
1 tsp chilli powder
1 tsp cumin powder
½ tsp coriander powder
1 tbsp coconut vinegar
½ tsp salt

2 tbsp oil
1 cup green masala (see p. 3)
Flesh of 6 green coconuts, cubed small
Salt to taste

- Mix ingredients for marinade, rub into oysters and marinate for 15 minutes.

- Place large pan on medium heat and add oil. When oil is hot, add green masala and coconut cubes. Fry for 3 minutes.

- Add oysters along with marinade and fry for 3 minutes. Cover and cook for 2 minutes.

- Serve hot with bhakri and koshimbir.

KESHARI DAHYATLI MACHHI

Saffron Pomfret

Serves 4

1 kg pomfret steaks, cleaned.

2 tbsp oil
½ tsp mustard seeds
6 green chillies, slit lengthwise
½ kg curd, beaten well
¼ tsp sugar
1 tsp saffron strands, soaked in 1 tbsp milk
Salt to taste

- Place flat-bottomed pan on medium heat. Add oil. When oil is hot, add mustard seeds and chillies. Fry for 1 minute.

- Add curd and fry for 1 minute. Add sugar, salt and fish steaks. Cover and cook on low heat for 10 minutes or until fish is done.

- Add saffron along with the milk. Put off heat and keep for 3 minutes.

- Serve hot with steamed rice.

PATICHA MADHE WAFAVLELI MACHHI

Steamed Fish with Lemon Grass

Serves 4-6

12 rawas steaks, cleaned.

6 tbsp lime juice
12 cloves garlic, peeled
12 green chillies, slit lengthwise
12 tbsp chopped fresh lemon grass leaf
1 tsp salt

Banana leaf, softened over low flame, or baking foil, cut into 12 pieces
4 tbsp oil, to grease banana leaf or foil

- Marinate fish in lime juice and salt for 15 minutes.

- Lightly grease each piece of banana leaf or foil. Place fish steak on it. Top each fish steak with 1 clove garlic and 1 slit green chilli and cover with 1 tbsp of lemon grass. Wrap individually and secure with toothpick.

- Grease baking tray and arrange fish steak packets on it. Bake in oven at 180°C (350°F) for 30 minutes.

- Serve hot with wrapping, as hors d'oeuvre.

AMBOSHITLI KOLAMBI

Prawn with Amboshi

Serves 4

This recipe may be made with heads of large prawns. The heads are chewed and discarded and the sauce is eaten with rice. It is extremely sour and will activate tastebuds.

24 whole prawns in shell, cleaned, with head and tail intact.

For marinade:

½ tsp turmeric powder
½ tsp lime juice
½ tsp salt

1 tsp oil
1 tbsp amboshi
½ tsp minced garlic
¼ tsp chilli powder
¼ tsp coriander powder
¼ tsp cumin powder
½ tsp sugar
1 tbsp tamarind purée
Salt to taste
1 tbsp chopped coriander leaves, to garnish

- Mix ingredients for marinade, rub into prawns and marinate for 15 minutes.

- Place flat-bottomed pan on medium heat and add oil. Before oil starts to smoke, add amboshi, garlic, powdered spices, sugar and salt. Fry for 2 minutes.

- Add marinated prawns along with marinade and 1 cup water. Cover and cook on low heat for 10 minutes. Add tamarind and a little water if necessary. Cover and cook for 5 minutes until very little gravy is left. Turn off heat and sprinkle with chopped coriander.

- Serve with freshly steamed rice.

KAJUTLI KALWA

Oyster in Cashew Cream

Serves 4

1 kg oysters, taken off the shell and cleaned.

For marinade:

1 tsp ginger
½ tsp garlic
1 tsp lime juice
½ tsp salt

1 tbsp rice flour
1 tbsp oil
2 dried red chillies, deseeded
1 cup ground unroasted cashewnuts
¼ tsp sugar
¼ tsp saffron strands, soaked in 1 tbsp water
Salt to taste

- Mix ingredients for marinade and rub into fish. Marinate for 15 minutes.

- Add some water to rice flour and blend into smooth paste. Set aside.

- Place flat-bottomed pan on medium heat and add oil. Before oil starts to smoke, add chillies and fry for 2 minutes. Add marinated oysters along with marinade. Fry for 1 minute. Add ground cashewnuts, with 1 cup water and cover.

- Cook on low heat for 5 minutes till oysters turn opaque. Add rice flour paste, sugar and ½ cup water, stirring constantly to ensure that flour does not coagulate. Gravy should have thick, creamy consistency. Turn off heat. Add soaked saffron along with water. Keep covered for 2 minutes.

- Serve hot with steamed rice.

130

DARUTLA SARANGA

Poached Pomfret in Feni

Serves 4-6

2 kg pomfret fillets, cleaned, skinned and deboned.

1½ cup coconut feni
1 tbsp ghee or butter
1 tsp minced garlic
1½ tbsp green peppercorns
1 tsp sugar
2 tbsp rice flour
Salt to taste
½ cup chopped coriander leaves, to garnish

- Rub in some salt on fish and place in shallow plate. Cover with feni and marinate for 15 minutes.

- Place large non-stick frying pan on medium heat and add ghee or butter. As soon as ghee melts, add garlic and green peppercorns and fry for 2 minutes. Add 2 cups water, sugar and salt and bring to boil.

- Add marinated fillets along with marinade. Cover and cook on low heat for 10 minutes till pomfret is done. Carefully remove fish fillets and lay on large serving plate.

- Add spoonful of gravy to rice flour and blend into a smooth paste. Add paste to juice in pan. Cook over medium heat for 3 minutes, stirring constantly to ensure that flour does not coagulate. Turn off heat and pour sauce over fish.

- Garnish with chopped coriander. Serve with steamed rice cakes.

TOMYATOTLI MACHHI

Tomato Fish

Serves 4

Fish that may be used are pomfret, surmai, rawas, bangda and boi.

1 kg fish steaks, cleaned. If using boi, clean and leave whole.

For marinade:

1 tsp turmeric powder
1 tsp lime juice
½ tsp salt

1 tbsp ghee or butter
4 black peppercorns
½ tsp grated ginger
1 tbsp minced garlic
¼ tsp chilli powder
¼ tsp cumin powder
4 medium-sized tomatoes, peeled (see p. 10) and diced
1 tbsp feni
Salt to taste
1 tbsp chopped coriander leaves, to garnish

- Mix ingredients for marinade, rub into fish and marinate for 15 minutes.

- Place flat-bottomed pan on medium heat and add ghee. When ghee melts, add peppercorns. When peppercorns start to splutter, add ginger, garlic, powdered spices and tomatoes. Fry for 3 minutes. Add 1 cup water, cover and cook for 5 minutes.

- Add marinated fish along with marinade and 2 cups water. Reduce heat, cover and cook for 10 minutes till fish is done and sauce is thick.

- Turn off heat and add feni. Keep covered for 2 minutes.

- Remove onto serving dish and discard peppercorns. Garnish with chopped coriander and serve with steamed rice.

KOLAMBICHI PEYJ

Prawn Kanji

Serves 4

4 cups small prawns, cleaned, shelled and steamed.

For marinade:

1 green chilli, finely chopped
1 tsp grated ginger
½ tsp minced garlic
1 tbsp lime juice
½ tsp salt

2 cups rice, broken or roughly pounded
1 tbsp lime juice
1 tsp sugar
1 tsp cumin seeds
6 tsp melted ghee or butter
½ tsp saffron, soaked in 1 tsp water
Salt to taste

- Mix ingredients for marinade, rub into prawns and marinate for 15 minutes.

- Put rice in deep pan and add water, twice the quantity of rice. Place on medium heat and boil until done. Add water and boil to achieve porridge consistency.

- Lower heat and add lime juice, sugar and salt. Mix well. Add marinated prawns along with marinade and mix thoroughly.

- Place small pan on high heat and add 2 tsp ghee or butter. Add cumin seeds. When cumin seeds start to splutter and turn brown, turn off heat. Add cumin seeds and ghee to porridge and mix.

- Increase heat and bring to boil. Turn off heat. Add saffron along with water. Cover for 2 minutes.

- Serve piping hot, in individual bowls and add 1 tsp of melted ghee to each serving.

AMSUL ANI MOTHI KOLAMBI

Amsul and King Prawn Stew

Serves 4

12 king prawns, cleaned and shelled.

For marinade:

2 tsp grated ginger
2 tsp minced garlic
2 green chillies, minced
2 tbsp lime juice
½ tsp salt

1 tbsp oil
1 tsp cumin seeds
24 whole spring onions, stems discarded
24 baby potatoes, peeled
1 tsp sugar
10 pods amsul, soaked in 2 cups water for 15 minutes
4 cups coconut milk of medium consistency
½ cup chopped coriander leaves
Salt to taste

- Mix ingredients for marinade and rub into prawns. Marinate for 15 minutes.

- Place large flat-bottomed pan on medium heat and add oil. Before oil starts to smoke, add cumin seeds. When cumin seeds start to splutter, add spring onions and potatoes. Add 2 cups water, cover and cook for 10 minutes.

- Add marinated prawns along with marinade and sugar. Cover and cook for 2 minutes.

- Add salt and amsul with its water. Mix and allow to cook for 5 minutes.

- Lower heat. Add coconut milk and coriander. Turn up heat and bring to quick boil. Turn off heat immediately.

- Serve with steamed rice.

KARANDI ANI KARLA

Karela with Dried Prawn

Serves 4

3 cups dried karandi, soaked in water for 10 minutes and washed thoroughly.

2 fresh karelas, 6" long
2 tbsp oil
6 curry leaves
2 large onions, chopped fine
1 tsp chilli powder
1 tsp coriander powder
1 tsp cumin powder
½ turmeric powder
2 tbsp crushed jaggery
4 tbsp tamarind purée
½ tsp garam masala powder
Salt to taste
2 tbsp chopped coriander leaves, to garnish

- Wash karelas, cut off and discard stem and ¼" of front end. Make very thin round slices and discard any ripe seeds. Soak slices in salted water for ½ hour. Wash thoroughly, drain and set aside.

- Place wok on medium heat and add oil. Before oil starts to smoke, add curry leaves. When curry leaves start to splutter, add onion and fry until dark brown.

- Add karela, powdered spices, jaggery, tamarind and salt. Fry for 5 minutes. Add dried prawn, mix well and fry for 3 minutes.

- Add 1 cup water, cover and cook for 10 minutes, checking if any extra water is required. Ensure that karela is cooked soft and preparation has a semi-dry consistency. Turn off fire, add garam masala and cover for 2 minutes.

- Garnish with chopped coriander and serve hot with bhakri.

SARANGA ANI PIKLELA AMBA

Pomfret and Ripe Mango

Serves 4

1 kg pomfret steaks, cleaned.

2 tbsp lime juice
2 tbsp oil
1 tsp black mustard seeds
4 curry leaves
2 dried red chillies, deseeded
3 ripe mangoes, peeled and cut into long slices
1 tbsp grated ginger
Salt to taste
1 tsp chopped coriander leaves, to garnish

- Rub 1 tbsp lime juice and some salt into fish. Marinate for 15 minutes.

- Place flat-bottomed pan on medium heat and add oil. Before oil starts to smoke, add mustard seeds, curry leaves and chillies. Fry till spices start to splutter. Add sliced mango, 1 tbsp lime juice and ginger. Fry for 2 minutes.

- Add marinated fish along with marinade. Add 1½ cups water. Cover and cook for 10 minutes or till fish is done. Turn off heat, remove and discard curry leaves and chillies.

- Garnish with coriander and serve hot in a shallow bowl. Serve with steamed toddy rice cakes.

KOLAMBICHA TIKHAT SHEERA

Spicy Sheera with Prawns

Serves 4

This makes a tasty teatime snack.

2 cups small prawns, cleaned and shelled.

For marinade:

1 tsp grated ginger
½ tsp turmeric powder
1 tbsp lime juice
½ tsp salt

3 cups coarse rawa
1 tbsp oil
6 curry leaves
4 black peppercorns
4 cloves
1" piece cinnamon
2 green chillies, chopped
1 large onion, chopped
¼ tsp mace or nutmeg powder
½ tsp garam masala powder
2 cups shelled green peas
Salt to taste
2 tbsp freshly grated coconut, to garnish
½ cup chopped coriander leaves, to garnish

- Mix ingredients for marinade, rub into prawns and marinate for 15 minutes.

- Place non-stick frying pan on medium heat. Add rawa, and dry roast, turning constantly until pink. Turn off heat and set aside.

- Place flat-bottomed pan on medium heat and add oil. Before oil starts to smoke, add curry leaves, peppercorns, cloves and cinnamon and fry. When spices start to splutter, add chilli, onion, mace or nutmeg powder and garam masala, and fry until onion is transparent.

- Add roasted rawa, green peas, 3 cups water and cook for 15 minutes, string constantly until dry. Make sure that rawa is cooked soft.

- Add marinated prawns along with marinade and a little water if necessary. Cook on low heat for 7 minutes, stirring constantly. Turn off heat, remove and discard curry leaves, peppercorns, cloves and cinnamon.

- Serve in individual bowls, garnished with chopped coriander and coconut.

DOUBLE BIYA ANI SHIMPLYA

Beans with Mussels

Serves 4

4 cups mussels, cleaned and shelled.

For marinade:

1 tsp grated ginger
1 tsp minced garlic
1 tbsp lime juice
½ tsp salt

1 tbsp oil
2 cups desiccated coconut
2 tbsp chopped coriander leaves
2 green chilli, diced
½ tsp cardamom powder
1 tsp cumin powder
½ tsp turmeric powder
4 cups fresh white kidney beans
½ tsp garam masala powder
Salt to taste

- Mix ingredients for marinade, rub into mussels and marinate in refrigerator for 20 minutes.

- Place flat-bottomed pan on medium heat and add oil. Before oil starts to smoke add coconut and fry until light brown. Add coriander, chilli and powdered spices, and fry for 2 minutes.

- Add kidney beans, salt and 3 cups water. Cover and cook till kidney beans are almost done.

- Add marinated mussels along with marinade and cook for 5 minutes till mussels are done and preparation is almost dry.

- Turn off heat, add garam masala and cover for 2 minutes.

- Serve hot with steamed rice cakes.

SHEVAIYA ANI SHIMPLYA

Spicy Spaghetti and Shellfish

Serves 4

Shevaiya is homemade wheat flour spaghetti. This may be substituted by ready-made shevaiya or spaghetti available in supermarkets. Assorted shellfish to be used together in this recipe are clam, mussel and oyster.

1½ cup clams, cleaned and shelled.
1½ cup mussels, cleaned and shelled.
1½ cup oysters, cleaned and shelled.

For marinade:

2 tsp grated ginger
2 tbsp feni
1 tbsp lime juice
½ tsp salt

For masala:

3 cups desiccated coconut
4 dried red chillies, deseeded and chopped
1 tbsp aniseed
1 tsp cumin seeds
16 cloves garlic, peeled
1" piece ginger, peeled and diced
4 cloves
1" piece cinnamon, broken into bits
2 tbsp lime juice
1 tsp sugar

3 tbsp oil

1½ packets long shevaiya or spaghetti
1 tbsp ghee or butter
1 cup feni
Salt to taste
1 cup chopped coriander leaves, to garnish

- Mix ingredients for marinade, and rub into shellfish. Marinate in the refrigerator for 20 minutes.

- Grind masala together in an electric mixer or with a hand grinder.

- Place frying pan on medium heat and add 1 tbsp oil. Before oil starts to smoke, add ground masala, lower heat and fry for 5 minutes, turning constantly. Turn off heat and set aside.

- Place flat-bottomed pan on medium heat and add 1 tbsp of oil. Before oil starts to smoke, add marinated shellfish along with marinade and salt. Lower heat and fry for 2 minutes.

- Add fried masala, mix well and fry for 5 minutes. Set aside.

- Break shevaiya or spaghetti into 4" pieces. Fill deep saucepan with salted water and 1 tbsp oil. When water boils, add shevaiya. Boil till done. Shevaiya must be firm when cooked and break with a little pressure between thumb and forefinger. Do not overcook till soft or they will get mashed during further cooking. Drain shevaiya in large sieve and set aside.

- Place large non-stick frying pan on medium heat and add butter or ghee. As soon as butter or ghee melts, add shevaiya, lower heat and fry for 5 minutes, tossing gently so as not to break them. Add shellfish masala mixture and mix well with wooden pasta forks. Turn off heat and add feni. Mix well.

- Serve in large decorative bowl, topped generously with chopped coriander.

NARLATLI CHIMBORI

Crab Claws in Coconut Cream

Serves 4

12 medium-sized crab claws, cleaned and prepared.

2 tsp sugar
1 tbsp butter or ghee
2 tsp grated ginger
2 cups coconut milk of thick consistency
6 green chillies, deseeded and cut into long strips
½ tsp garam masala powder
2 tbsp feni
Salt to taste

- Boil water in deep saucepan on high heat. Add crab claws and boil for 10 minutes. Turn off heat and remove from pan.

- Cool crab under running water and crack open. Discard shell. Carefully separate each part at joint without flaking. Set aside.

- Place non-stick frying pan on medium heat and add 4 tbsps water and sugar. Caramelize. When liquid starts turning brown, add ½ cup water and butter or ghee. Mix well.

- When butter or ghee melts, add crab claws and ginger. Sauté for 7 minutes. Add coconut milk, chillies, salt and garam masala. When liquid starts bubbling, turn off heat and allow to cool for 5 minutes. Add feni.

- Serve with steamed rice cakes.

BAKED NISTE

Baked Masala Fish

Serves 4-6

This is a popular South Indian dish. Fish that may be used are gol fish, surmai and rawas.

12 fish steaks, cleaned.

1 tsp turmeric powder
Oil, for frying
2 large onions, chopped
10 peppercorns, crushed
3 green chillies, chopped
1 tbsp garlic paste
1" piece fresh ginger, diced
1 tsp chilli powder
1 tsp cumin powder
½ coriander powder
½ tsp clove powder
½ tsp cinnamon powder
8 curry leaves
2 large tomatoes, peeled (see p. 10) and chopped
2 tbsp vinegar
Salt to taste

- Rub in ½ tsp salt and turmeric powder on fish and marinate for 15 minutes.

- Put oil on medium heat in frying pan. Fry chopped onions until transluscent. Add all other ingredients and fry till cooked. Set aside to cool. Divide the cooked masala into 2 portions

- Grease baking pan with oil. Spread one portion of masala, on baking pan. Gently arrange marinated fish steaks on bed of masala. Cover fish with remaining masala. Cover baking pan with lid or baking foil.

- Pre-heat oven to 180°C (350°F). Bake for 30 minutes. Baste fish with oil if necessary so that it does not turn dry.

- Serve with thick slices of white bread or with rice.

MANKYO MASALA

Squid Dry Masala

Serves 4

This is a delicious Goan dish.

> 750 gms squid, cleaned and cut into rings.

For marinade:

> 1 tbsp grated ginger
> 1 tbsp garlic paste
> 1 tbsp coconut vinegar
> ½ tsp cumin powder
> ½ tsp coriander powder
> 1 tsp chilli powder
> 1 tsp turmeric powder
>
> 1 tbsp oil
> 2 large onions, chopped
> 1 large tomato, peeled (see p. 10) and diced
> 8 curry leaves
> Salt to taste

- Rub all ingredients for marinade into squid and marinate for 30 minutes.

- Heat oil on medium heat in frying pan. Add onion and fry till transluscent. Add tomato and curry leaves and fry lightly.

- Add squid with marinade. Cover frying pan and cook on low heat for 15 minutes. Do not overcook squid or else it will turn rubbery and inedible.

- Serve with thick slices of white bread.

ILLISH MACHH BHAPÉ

Steamed Hilsa in Mustard

Serves 4

(Recipe courtesy Sangeeta Sengupta)

Hilsa is a river fish found only in the river Ganges in India and in the river Padma in Bangladesh. It is a common belief that the hilsa from the river Padma is tastier. This is a large fish and should be eaten carefully as it has a lot of bones. This recipe comes from Bengal.

8 large hilsa steaks, cleaned.

4 tbsp yellow mustard seeds
8 green chillies
4 tbsp mustard oil
Salt to taste

Banana leaf, softened over a low flame and cut into 8 pieces
8 cloves

- Grind yellow mustard seeds and green chillies to fine paste. Add mustard oil to paste and mix thoroughly.

- Rub salt and paste over each piece of fish and marinate for 30 minutes.

- Wrap fish steaks individually in banana leaf pieces and secure each with a clove.

- Steam fish parcels in flat-bottomed steamer for 20 minutes.

- Serve with freshly steamed rice.

GODAK

Fish Cooked in Bamboo

Serves 2

This recipe is from Tripura.

2 small river trout, cleaned and left whole.
8 large prawns, shelled and cleaned.

1 large potato with skin, cubed
1 raw banana with skin, cubed
2 cups banana flowers, chopped
2 drumsticks, chopped into 8 pieces
2 tsp turmeric powder
4 whole green chillies
2 large onions, sliced
Salt to taste

2' hollow bamboo, 4" diameter, closed at bottom
Banana leaves for sealing bamboo

- Make a small open fire with charcoal and sticks.
- Wash bamboo thoroughly. Stuff bamboo with potatoes, bananas, banana flowers and drumsticks.
- Put in the trout and prawns. Add turmeric powder, chillies, salt and sliced onions. Pack ingredients tightly, pressing in with fingers.
- Take banana leaves and stuff in the opening to seal it.

- Stand the bamboo slanting against the open fire. Keep turning till it is charred well on all sides.

- Remove banana leaves and pour contents on large plate. It will be of stew consistency.

- Serve with steamed rice. Langi or kanchi, the local rice wine is drunk with this.

PATRA NI MACHHI

Pomfret in Banana Leaf

Serves 6

(Recipe courtesy Bhikoo Manekshaw)

This is the most popular of all Parsi fish preparations.

12 pomfret steaks, cleaned and sliced ½" thick through the bone.

1 tbsp lime juice

For coconut chutney:
1 coconut, grated
6 green chillies, deseeded
6 tbsp chopped coriander leaves
1 tbsp chopped mint leaves
1½ " piece ginger, peeled and chopped
2 cloves garlic, peeled
½ tsp turmeric powder
1 tsp cumin powder
Juice of 2 limes
Salt to taste

Banana leaf, softened by holding over low flame and cut into 12 pieces
2 tbsp oil, for baking

- Marinate fish with lime juice and ½ tsp salt for 30 minutes.

- Grind chutney ingredients with a little water in an electric mixer or with a hand grinder.

- Spread chutney on both sides of each piece of fish.

- Wrap each piece in a piece of banana leaf like a parcel. Tie each parcel with cotton thread.

- Place fish in a large steamer and steam for 20 minutes.

- Alternatively, bake in an oven at 180°C (350°F). Put ½" water mixed with oil in a tray and place fish in it. Put tray into oven and bake for 15 minutes.

- When fish is cooked, remove string.

- Serve hot in a banana wrapping.

AMLI NE MACHHI NO PATIO

Tamarind and Fish Patio

Serves 2-3

(Recipe courtesy Bhicoo Manekshaw)

This is a delightful Parsi dish.

500 gm pomfret or any other fish steaks, sliced ½" thick through the
bone, or prawns, shelled and cleaned.

2 tsp cumin seeds
1 large clove garlic, peeled
1-2 tsp chilli powder or 6 dried red chillies
1 tbsp vinegar
1 tsp turmeric powder
Oil, for frying
Tamarind, the size of a lime, infused in 2 cups water
2 tsp sugar
Salt to taste

- Rub fish with a little salt and keep aside for 30 minutes.

- Grind cumin seeds, garlic and chillies in vinegar. Add turmeric. Rub half the ground spices on fish.

- Heat oil in pan and fry remaining spices. Add fish and sauté for a minute.

- Strain tamarind water into pan, add sugar and salt and simmer on medium heat till fish is done and gravy is thick.

- Serve with steamed rice and dal.

Titbits and Salads

MACHHICHE CUTLET

Fish Cutlets

Serves 4

2 cups boiled pomfret, rawas or surmai, flaked, or cooked prawns,
shelled and chopped.

3 cups potatoes, boiled and mashed coarsely
1 tsp grated ginger
2 green chillies, finely chopped
1 cup chopped coriander leaves
2 tsp lime juice
¼ tsp nutmeg powder
4 slices of bread, edges trimmed, dipped in cold water, squeezed and
crumbled
Whites of 6 eggs, beaten with 1 tbsp water
2 cups dry breadcrumbs
4 tbsp oil, for frying
Salt to taste

- Mix all ingredients, except bread slices, breadcrumbs, egg and oil.

- Add crumbled bread to fish mixture and knead so that it forms a homogenous mass. Divide into 4 equal portions.

- On greased surface, roll out each portion evenly to 2" thickness with greased rolling pin. Using medium-sized cutlet cutters, make 8 cutlets.

- Dip each cutlet in egg-white mixture.

- Spread out dry breadcrumbs on flat surface and coat each cutlet on either side and on the edges.

- Heat oil in non-stick frying pan at medium heat. Fry cutlets on both sides until golden brown.

- Serve hot with tomato chutney or ketchup.

ANDYATLI MACHHI

Fish Angels

Serves 12

These make tasty hors d'oeuvres.

2 cups boiled pomfret, rawas or surmai, flaked, or cooked prawns, chopped.

12 large eggs, hard-boiled and halved
2 cups boiled potatoes, mashed coarsely
1 tsp grated ginger
1 tsp green chilli, finely chopped
4 tbsp fresh cream
¼ tsp nutmeg powder
2 cups dry breadcrumbs or grated cheese
Salt to taste

- Gently twist each half of egg to separate yolk from white. Preserve yolk for other use. Keep hollow whites aside.

- Mix all other ingredients, except breadcrumbs or cheese, together. Knead to form a homogenous mass.

- Fill hollow egg whites with mixture and level flat. Top with dry breadcrumbs or grated cheese and grill for 7 minutes until golden.

- Serve hot on a bed of koshimbir.

KOLAMBICHYA KARANJYA

Prawn Karanjis

Makes 12

Prawn karanjis make a tasty teatime snack. Baby-sized karanjis may be served with cocktails. Modaks or dumplings and vol-au-vents can also be made with the same filling.

2 cups small prawns, cleaned.

For marinade:

1 tsp grated ginger
¼ minced garlic
1 tsp lime juice
½ tsp salt

Oil, for frying
1 medium onion, chopped
2 green chillies, diced
1 tbsp chopped coriander leaves
2 cups rice flour
Salt to taste

- Mix marinade and rub into prawns. Marinate for 15 minutes.

- Place flat-bottomed pan on medium heat and add 1 tsp oil. Before oil starts to smoke, add onion and fry until transparent. Add chillies and fry for 3 minutes.

- Add marinated prawns along with marinade and salt. Put on very low heat, cover and cook for 5 minutes until prawns are done and the mixture is completely dry.

- Add chopped coriander and mix well. Turn off heat and set aside. Allow to cool to room temperature.

- Prepare dough with rice flour, a little oil and water, and roll out pancakes of 4" diameter. Grease one side of pancake and spoon prawn mixture on it, covering only half the pancake. Fold other half of pancake over filling and press down, bringing both edges together.

- Cut round edges evenly with pastry cutter. The karanjis are now ready for frying.

- Place wok on medium heat and add enough oil to deep-fry. Before oil starts to smoke, put in karanjis and fry till golden brown. Remove on absorbent paper to drain excess oil.

- Serve with sweet and sour mango chutney.

For modaks or dumplings:

- Use same prawn filling. Roll out pancake as indicated and spoon mixture in centre of pancake.

- Lift edges and press together on top in a point. Steam for 20 minutes.

For vol-au-vents:

- Use same prawn filling. Loosely pack filling in vol-au-vent shells, which are available ready-made at delicatessens.

- Mix grated cheese and dry breadcrumbs together and sprinkle on top. Grill for 7 minutes until golden brown on top.

KOLAMBI ANI KANSACHI BHUJJI

Prawn and Sweet Corn Fritters

Makes 12

2 cups prawns, boiled, shelled and roughly diced.

2 cups fresh sweet corn, boiled and ground
2 green chillies, diced
1 tsp grated ginger
½ tsp minced garlic
1 tbsp chopped green dill
2 slices of bread, edges trimmed, soaked in cold water for a minute,
squeezed dry and crumbled
1 tsp lime juice
White of 6 eggs, beaten with 1 tbsp water
2 cups dry breadcrumbs
Oil, for frying
Salt to taste

- Mix all ingredients, except breadcrumbs, eggs and oil, together to form a dough. Divide into 12 equal parts. Roll each part by hand on greased surface to form a thick roll 3" in length.

- Dip each fritter in egg-white mixture.

- Spread dry breadcrumbs on flat surface. Roll fritter on crumbs and coat completely.

- Place non-stick frying pan on medium heat and add oil. Shallow-fry fritters till golden brown.

- Serve hot with tomato chutney or ketchup.

KOLAMBICHA POLA

Prawn Pancakes with Spicy Coconut Milk

Makes 4

This makes a sumptuous breakfast.

> 1 cup small prawns, shelled, boiled and chopped.

For pancakes:
> 1 tsp lime juice
> 1 green chilli, chopped
> ½ tsp grated ginger
> ½ tsp minced garlic
> 1 pinch mace or nutmeg powder
> 1 cup rice flour
> 1 tsp oil
> Salt to taste

For spicy coconut milk:
> ¼ tsp black mustard seeds
> 1 green chilli, slit lengthwise
> 2 cups coconut milk of medium consistency
> ½ tsp sugar
> 1 tsp chopped coriander leaves
> 1 tsp oil
> Salt to taste

- Marinate prawns in lime juice and some salt for 15 minutes.
- Mix prawns with all other pancake ingredients, except rice flour and oil, and set aside.

- Add oil and water to rice flour and make a soft dough. Add prawn mixture to dough and knead well. Divide into 4 parts. With rolling pin, roll out 4 pancakes of ¼" thickness on a greased surface.

- Steam for 20 minutes.

For spicy coconut milk:

- Place flat-bottomed pan on medium heat and add oil. Before oil starts to smoke, add mustard seeds. When mustard seeds start to splutter, add chilli. Fry for 2 minutes.

- Add coconut milk, sugar, chopped coriander and salt. Bring to boil, turn off heat and cover.

- Serve hot pancakes with individual bowls of spicy coconut milk. Pancakes are eaten dipped in coconut milk.

MACHHICHE ROLL

Pomfret Roll

Makes 4

This makes an elegant hors d'oeuvre.

2 pomfret fillets, cleaned.

For marinade:

1 tsp grated ginger
1 tsp minced garlic
1 green chilli, minced
1 pinch mace or nutmeg powder
½ tsp salt

2 large spinach leaves, washed in salted water and wiped dry
2 cups Kolam rice or any small grained sticky rice, steamed
Salt to taste

- Cut pomfret fillets to size of spinach leaves.

- Mix ingredients for marinade and rub into fish. Marinate for 15 minutes. Steam fish and set aside.

- Lay spinach leaves on a chopping board. Cut off stems. Spoon and spread rice on each spinach leaf upto ¼" thickness, leaving ½" uncoated from either end. Lay steamed fish lengthwise, one on each leaf.

- Cut leaves in half with a sharp knife, making 4 portions. Roll each piece from cut end and secure with wooden toothpick.

- Steam for 7 minutes till spinach leaf is cooked. Do not overcook or the leaf will lose its bright green colour and will droop.

- Cool to room temperature and serve bunched together on a small bamboo plate.

MACHHICHE GOLEY

Fish Marbles

Makes 12

This is a good accompaniment to cocktails.

2 cups red chilli fried fish, flaked and carefully deboned (see p. 63).

3 cups Kolam or any small-grained rice, steamed
2 tbsp tomato purée
1 tsp coconut feni
Salt to taste

- Mix ingredients together, taking care not to crush the grains of rice. Divide into 12 equal parts. Grease palms and form 12 perfectly round balls from mixture.

- Arrange in greased baking dish and grill for 7 minutes. Turn the balls over and grill for 7 minutes.

- Serve hot.

KOLAMBICHA OMELETTE

Prawn Omelette with Curd Chutney

Serves 4

This make a sumptuous breakfast.

1 cup small prawns, shelled and cleaned.

For marinade:

½ tsp grated ginger
½ tsp minced garlic
½ tsp turmeric
1 tsp lime juice
½ tsp salt

For omelette:

½ cup rice flour
1 cup gram flour
1 medium onion, chopped
1 green chilli, chopped
1 tbsp chopped coriander leaves
½ tsp chilli powder
¼ tsp garam masala powder
Salt to taste
1 tbsp oil, for frying each omelette

For curd chutney:

1½ cups curd
1 pinch cardamom powder
½ tsp grated ginger
½ tsp sugar
¼ salt
2 curry leaves
1 whole dried red chilli, deseeded
¼ tsp black mustard seeds

For omelette:

- Mix ingredients for marinade, rub into prawns and marinate for 15 minutes.

- Mix ingredients for omelette together, except oil. Add water to form smooth paste.

- Add marinated prawns along with marinade and a little water to form thick liquid consistency. Divide into 4 parts.

- Place non-stick frying pan on medium heat and add oil. Before oil starts to smoke, pour in mixture for 1 omelette. Fry for 3 minutes.

- Reduce heat to minimum, cover and cook for 10 minutes. Turn omelette over. Add oil to pan if necessary and cook for 5 minutes until done. Keep hot.

For curd chutney:

- Blend curd to a smooth paste with a hand mixer. Add cardamom powder, ginger, sugar and salt. Mix well till sugar melts.

- Place pan on medium heat and add oil. Before oil starts to smoke, add curry leaves, red chilli and mustard seeds. Fry for 2 minutes.

- When spices start to splutter, reduce heat and gently pour in curd mixture. Take care it does not splash. Cook for 3 minutes, stirring constantly. Turn off heat. Remove and discard curry leaves and red chilli.

- Serve hot omelettes with curd chutney in individual bowls. Omelettes are eaten dipped in chutney.

MACHHICHI KOSHIMBIR

Fish Salad

Serves 4

4 cups steamed rawas or surmai, in ½" cubes.
4 cups medium-sized prawns, shelled and steamed.

For marinade:

1 tbsp lime juice
1 pinch mace or nutmeg powder
¼ tsp sugar
1 tbsp oil
½ tsp salt

4 cups watermelon, cubed
1 medium onion, chopped finely
1 tsp grated ginger
1 tsp chopped garlic
1 green chilli, diced
1 tbsp chopped coriander leaves
1 capsicum, sliced, to garnish
1 medium tomato, quartered, to garnish

- Mix ingredients for marinade. In glass salad bowl, add steamed fish and watermelon to marinade. Mix well. Marinate for 15 minutes.

- Mix onion, ginger, garlic, chilli and chopped coriander and keep for 15 minutes. Add mixture to fish and mix gently, taking care not to break fish.

- Garnish with long slices of capsicum and tomato quarters and serve in individual salad plates on hot baby-sized rice flour bhakris.

MODKACHI BHUJJI

Whitebait Hors D'oeuvre

Serves 4

750 gm whitebait, cleaned.

For marinade:

1 tbsp grated ginger
½ cup feni
2 tbsp lime juice
½ tsp sugar
1 tsp oil
½ tsp salt

For batter:

1½ cups rice flour
1 tbsp chopped coriander leaves
Oil, for frying
Salt to taste

Spring onions, to garnish

- Mix ingredients for marinade and add to fish. Refrigerate for 6 hours.

- Mix rice flour with coriander, water and salt and prepare thick batter.

- Heat oil in wok.

- Dip each fish in batter, coat well and deep-fry in hot oil until golden brown and crisp. Remove on absorbent paper and allow oil to drain.

- Ganish with spring onions.

KOLAMBI ANI AMBYACHI KOSHIMBIR

Prawn and Ripe Mango Salad

Serves 4-6

4 cups medium-sized prawns, cleaned, shelled and steamed.

For marinade:

1½ tbsp grated ginger
2 tbsp lime juice
½ tsp salt

8 cups ripe mango, peeled and cubed
Flesh of 2 large green coconuts cut into ½" squares
1 tbsp chopped coriander leaves
1 tbsp freshly ground black pepper
1 tbsp feni
Salt to taste

- Mix ingredients for marinade, rub into prawns and marinate for 15 minutes.

- Mix together mango cubes, coconut and marinated prawns along with marinade. Add coriander, pepper and feni, and mix well, taking care not to mash mango cubes.

- Serve salad in individual salad bowls, accompanied by hot baby-sized bhakris.

TALLELYA KALWAVAR ANDE

Sunny Egg on Oyster

Serves 1-2

1 cup baby oysters, shelled and cleaned.

For marinade:

½ tsp turmeric powder
2 tsp lime juice
½ tsp salt

½ tsp grated ginger
½ tsp minced garlic
½ tsp coriander powder
½ cumin powder
½ chilli powder
½ tsp garam masala powder
1 tsp crushed jaggery
2 tbsp chopped coriander leaves
1 medium onion, chopped
1 tbsp oil
2 large eggs
Salt to taste
Additional chopped coriander leaves, to garnish

- Mix ingredients for marinade, rub into oysters and marinate for 15 minutes. Divide into 2 portions.

- Mix all other ingredients, except onion, oil and eggs, and divide into 2 portions.

- Place non-stick flat frying pan on medium heat and add oil. Preferably use non-stick frying pan 5" in diameter, especially available for frying eggs individually.

- Before oil starts to smoke, add half the onion and fry until brown. Add one portion of oysters and other mixed ingredients. Fry well until oysters turn opaque.

- Mass the fried mixture in centre of pan and flatten with a wooden spatula until 5" round in diameter. Break egg deftly over mixture, so that yolk remains perfectly in the centre. No extra oil is required.

- Once white of egg is cooked turn heat off and cover for 2 minutes. Remove deftly in the centre of a medium-sized plate. Garnish with chopped coriander.

- Repeat with the other portion.

- Serve with hot baby-sized bhakris.

KARANDI ANI BATYATYACHEY BALL

Potato and Dried Prawn Balls

Makes 4

1 cup dried karandi, washed and soaked in cold water for 10 minutes.

For marinade:

½ tsp turmeric
1 tsp lime juice
½ tsp salt

2 large potatoes, boiled, peeled and mashed
2 slices of white bread, edges trimmed, dipped in cold water, squeezed and crumbled
1 pinch mace or nutmeg powder
1 tbsp oil, for the stuffing
1 medium onion, chopped
1 green chilli, chopped
1 tsp crumbled jaggery
½ tsp grated ginger
¼ tsp garam masala powder
1 tbsp chopped coriander leaves
½ cup dry breadcrumbs
Additional oil, for frying
Salt to taste
Spring onions, to garnish

- Mix ingredients for marinade and rub into fish. Marinate for 15 minutes.

- Add salt, mace or nutmeg and crumbled bread to potatoes. Knead into a dough. Divide into 4 parts.

- On greased surface, roll out each part with greased rolling pin into pancake about ¼" thick. Set aside.

- Place flat-bottomed pan on medium heat and add 1 tbsp oil. Before oil starts to smoke, add onion and fry until brown. Add remaining ingredients, except breadcrumbs, and marinated karandi along with its marinade. Fry well for 15 minutes till karandi is cooked. Set aside and allow to cool to room temperature.

- Divide karandi mixture into 4 portions. Grease palms and place one potato pancake on left palm. Spoon one portion of karandi mixture in centre and deftly curl pancake around, sealing it at the top to form a perfect ball.

- Spread dry breadcrumbs on even surface and roll the ball over breadcrumbs to cover evenly.

- Place wok on high heat and add oil for deep-frying. Before oil starts to smoke, add potato balls and fry until golden brown. Remove on absorbent paper, and allow oil to drain.

- Garnish with thin slivers of spring onion.

KISMIS ANI KALWA

Oysters and Sultana Hors D'oeuvre

Serves 4

4 large oysters, shelled and cleaned.

For marinade:

1 tsp grated ginger
1 tbsp lime juice
¼ tsp salt
1 pinch mace or nutmeg powder

For masala:

1 tbsp oil
½ cup sultanas
1 large onion, sliced
1 level tsp grated ginger
1 tbsp lime juice
¼ tsp garam masala powder
1 tsp sugar
Salt to taste

For batter:

½ cup rice flour
1 tbsp chopped green dill

Oil, for frying

- Mix ingredients for marinade, rub into fish and marinate in the refrigerator for 20 minutes.

- Place frying pan on medium heat and add oil. Before oil starts to smoke, add sultanas and fry till they swell up. Add onion and fry until transparent. Add ginger, lime juice, garam masala and salt, and fry for 5 minutes. Set aside.

- Place flat-bottomed pan on medium heat. Add 2 tbsp water. When water is heated, add 1 tsp sugar and caramelize. When liquid turns brown, add onion and sultana mixture immediately and mix well. Turn off heat and set aside.

- Make very thick batter with rice flour, chopped dill and water. Dip each oyster, covered with its marinade into batter and coat thickly.

  Place wok on high heat and add oil for deep-frying. Before oil starts to smoke, lower heat to medium, put oysters in and deep-fry until golden brown and done. Remove onto absorbent paper, and allow oil to drain.

- Heat sultana mixture until piping hot. Divide into 4 portions. Place 3" diameter biscuit cutter in centre of hors d'oeuvres plate. Spoon in 1 part of mixture and level with back of a teaspoon.

- Carefully remove biscuit cutter so as not to disturb the perfectly round shape. Place a fried oyster on top of each portion.

- Serve hot with baby-sized bhakris.

CHUTNEY ANI MACHHICHE SANDWICH

Pomfret and Chutney Cocktail Savory

Serves 4

2 large pomfret fillets, cleaned and steamed.

1 cup green masala (see p. 3)
White of 6 eggs
½ cup chopped coriander leaves
Oil, for deep-frying
Salt to taste

- Place fillets on wooden chopping board and, with greased sharp knife, cut into 2" squares. Slice each square into 2 parts.

- Add salt to the green masala and spoon chutney evenly on one part of each square. Cover top with other part, making a sandwich.

- Pour egg whites in shallow bowl and add 1 tbsp water and chopped coriander. Beat lightiy with fork.

- Place wok on high heat and add oil. Before oil starts to smoke, dip each sandwich in egg-white mixture and fry until golden brown.

- Serve hot as accompaniment to cocktails.

MACHHI ANI KISMIS CHI KOSHIMBIR

Sultana, Curd and Fish Salad

Serves 4

500 gm rawas or surmai, cubed and steamed with salt to taste.

200 gm brown sultanas, soaked and drained
500 gm curd, beaten with hand mixer
½ tsp chilli powder
½ tsp cumin powder
1 tsp roasted black sesame seeds
½ tsp salt
1 tsp sugar
1 cup chopped coriander, to garnish

- Take large decorative salad bowl and add all other ingredients, except fish and coriander. Mix thoroughly.

- Add fish cubes and gently cover with mixture. Be careful that cubes do not flake. Cover and refrigerate for 15 minutes.

- Garnish with chopped coriander and serve cool with hot bhakris.

MACHHICHI PLATE

Seafood Platter

Serves 4

12 king prawns, cleaned and shelled.
4 large pomfret steaks, cleaned.
1 kg large oysters, cleaned.
1 kg squid, cleaned and sliced round.
1 kg rawas cubes, cleaned.

For marinade:

1 cup coconut vinegar
1 tsp garlic paste
1 tbsp ginger paste
1 tbsp sugar
1 cup coconut feni
6 cloves, slightly bruised
1" piece cinnamon
Salt to taste

8 lime wedges, to garnish
1 cup chopped coriander leaves, to garnish

- Mix ingredients for marinade and keep for 2 hours.
- Put shellfish in large bowl. Add salt and mix.
- Put pomfret steaks and rawas cubes in separate bowl. Add salt and mix.
- Divide marinade and add to each bowl of fish.
- Steam shellfish for 7 minutes and fish for 10 minutes separately. Cover and refrigerate for 2 hours.

- Drain marinade and serve the seafood chilled, garnished with fresh coriander and lime wedges in large dish.

- Serve with triangles of fresh wheat or granary bread and homemade white butter. Chilled coconut water blended with 1 tbsp coconut feni and a dash of angostura bitters makes a good accompaniment.

COLMI NA KABAB

Prawn Kababs

Serves 4

(Recipe courtesy Bhicoo Manekshaw)

This is a typical Parsi dish.

500 gms prawns, cleaned and shelled.

2 onions, chopped, fried and well-drained
3 green chillies, deseeded and chopped
6 cloves garlic, chopped
1 tsp turmeric powder
1 chilli powder
1 tsp cumin powder
1 tbsp dhan sakh masala powder
1 egg, beaten
Lime juice to taste
Sesame seed oil, for frying
Salt to taste
Lime wedges, to garnish

- Blanche and coarsely chop prawns.
- Mix with remaining ingredients, taking care to add just enough egg to bind kababs. Shape into kababs and shallow-fry.
- Garnish with slices of lime.

Chutneys and Pickles

KOLAMBICHA GODAMBA

Sweet and Sour Prawn and Mango Chutney

Makes 3 kg

1 kg medium-sized prawns, cleaned, shelled and marinated in ½ tsp
salt.

1 kg crushed jaggery
10 roasted green chillies, slit and deseeded
1 tsp cumin seeds
1 tsp roasted aniseed
1 tbsp chilli powder
1 tsp roasted black sesame seeds
1 kg raw green mangoes, peeled, deseeded and cubed
4 cups coconut vinegar
Salt to taste

- Place wide non-stick pan on medium heat. Add
  jaggery and 4 cups water and cook to smooth soup
  consistency, stirring constantly.

- Lower heat and add all other ingredients, except
  prawns and vinegar. Stir and cook till mixture just
  starts thickening.

- Drain all moisture from prawns, add to mixture and
  cook for 5 minutes. Pour vinegar and cook on
  medium heat till mixture is thick and syrupy.

- Store in air-tight jar. It can be stored for 15 days.

KALVACHEY MULYATLEY LONCHEY

Fresh Oyster and Radish Pickle
Makes 1 kg

500 gm baby oysters, cleaned and prepared.

500 gm white radish, cut into small cubes
1 tsp turmeric powder
3 tsp mustard seeds
2 tsp amchur
2 tsp chilli powder
2 tsp sugar
4 tbsp oil
1 tsp cumin seeds
¼ tsp asafoetida powder
Salt to taste

- Mix oysters and chopped radish in large bowl. Add turmeric, 2 tsp mustard seeds and salt, and rub in thoroughly. Keep for 1 hour.

- Add amchur, chilli powder and sugar to the mixture and mix well. Add 2 tbsp water.

- Place pan on high heat. Add oil. When oil is hot, add cumin seeds, 1 tsp mustard seeds and asafoetida powder. When spices start to splutter, add oyster and radish mixture and stir. Cook for 5 minutes.

- Lower heat to medium, stir and cook for another 5 minutes. Turn off heat, cover and keep for about 6 hours.

- This pickle should be eaten fresh, but can be stored for upto 2 days in a refrigerator.

JAWLYACHI CHUTNEY

Garlic and Prawn Chutney

Makes 500 gm

500 gm prawns, cleaned and prepared.

6 tbsp oil
10 curry leaves
½ tsp asafoetida powder
2 tsp mustard seed
2 tsp cumin seed
2 tsp turmeric powder
2 cups tamarind purée
4 tsp chilli powder
4 large cloves garlic, peeled and chopped
Salt to taste

- Place pan on medium heat and add oil. When oil is hot, add curry leaves, asafoetida, mustard seeds, cumin seeds and turmeric. Fry for 1 minute.

- Add tamarind and cook for 2 minutes. Add chilli powder and salt, and simmer for 2 minutes.

- Add garlic and prawns, cover and cook for 10 minutes.

- Allow to cool and store in air-tight jar. This chutney should be refrigerated and eaten within a week.

MITHATLI KOLAMBI

Pickled Prawns

Makes 5 cupfuls

500 gm small prawns, cleaned, shelled and steamed.

4 cups coconut vinegar
10 green chillies, slit lengthwise
10 fresh red chillies, slit lengthwise
10 cloves garlic, peeled and chopped
2 pieces ginger, 1" each, peeled and chopped
½ tsp salt
½ tsp sugar

- Dry large air-tight jar and set aside.
- Mix all ingredients in bowl.
- Pour into jar. Shut lid tightly. Keep overnight or for a day.
- Refrigerate and eat within a week.

SUKYACHI CHUTNEY

Dried Fish Chutney I

Makes 1 cupful

1 cup dried and flaked rawas or surmai or gol, washed and soaked in
cold water for 10 minutes.

8 cloves garlic, peeled
1 tbsp desiccated coconut, dry roasted
2 dry roasted red chillies, deseeded and cut
2 tsp sesame seeds, dry roasted
½ tsp sugar
1 tsp oil
Salt to taste

- Place non-stick pan on low heat and dry-roast the
  fish and garlic for 5 minutes. Remove and set aside.

- Mix all ingredients, except oil, together and grind in
  an electric mixer or with a hand grinder. Keep in a
  bowl.

- Place non-stick frying pan on low heat. Add 1 tsp oil
  and grease pan completely. Add ground chutney
  and roast for 10 minutes, stirring constantly with
  wooden spatula. Turn off heat and allow to cool in
  pan to room temperature.

- Store in air-tight jar. This chutney lasts for 3 weeks
  in a refrigerator.

ONAKKA MEEN CHAMANDI

Dried Fish Chutney II

Makes 250 gm

This South Indian chutney can be made using any dried fish, cut into ½" small pieces or whole dried prawns.

250 gm dried fish, cleaned and soaked in cold water for 10 minutes.

4 dried red chillies, deseeded
1 clove
2 tbsp desiccated coconut
1 tsp cumin powder
1 tsp chopped garlic
1 tsp tamarind purée
1 tsp oil
Salt to taste

- Heat oil on low heat in frying pan. Add chillies, clove and desiccated coconut and fry for 2 minutes. Remove from fire and grind in an electric mixer or with a hand grinder.

- Return mixture again to frying pan. Add cumin, garlic and tamarind. Fry for 3 minutes and add dried fish. Mix well. Dry roast for 5 minutes. Remove from fire and allow to cool.

- Preserve in an air-tight jar. This chutney lasts for 3 weeks in a refrigerator.

KALLUMAKKAI

Oyster Pickle

Makes 500 gm

Other fish that may be used in this typically South Indian recipe are prawns and clams shelled.

500 gm baby oysters, cleaned and shelled.

½ tsp turmeric powder
4 dried red chillies
4 green chillies
1 tsp cumin seeds
1 tsp coriander seeds
1 tsp mustard seeds
8 peppercorns
½" piece ginger, chopped
6 cloves garlic, peeled and chopped
1 tbsp lime juice
2 tbsp oil
Salt to taste

- Marinate fish for 15 minutes with turmeric and ½ tsp salt.

- Grind all other ingredients, except oil, in an electric mixer or with a hand grinder, adding no water.

- Place flat-bottomed pan on medium heat and add oil. Before oil starts to smoke, add ground ingredients and fry for 3 minutes.

- Add marinated fish and fry for 5 minutes. Cover and cook for 5 minutes or until done. Do not overcook shellfish or it will be rubbery and inedible.

- Allow to cool and pour in an air-tight jar. This can be preserved upto 4 weeks in a refrigerator.

Accompaniments

BHAT

Steamed Rice

Serves 4

250 gm Kolam or small-grained rice, washed
¼ tsp salt
½ tsp oil

- Put rice in a flat-bottomed pan and gently pour water, double the level of rice, over it. Add salt and oil.

- Let rice boil for 5 minutes on high heat. Then reduce heat to minimum and cover with lid. Cook for about 10 minutes, till water evaporates.

- To check whether rice is cooked, take a grain of rice between thumb and forefinger. It should crush with a little pressure.

- Serve hot.

WAFLELYA BHATACHI MOOD

Steamed Rice Cakes with Toddy

Serves 4

250 gm rice flour
2 cups toddy
¼ tsp salt

- Mix all ingredients to form a thick paste. Cover and leave overnight.
- Next morning, mix well and pour into small metal bowls or an idli steamer and steam for 10 minutes.
- Serve hot.

WAFLELYA BHATACHI GODI MOOD

Sweet Steamed Rice Cakes with Toddy and Coconut

Serves 4

250 gm rice flour
2 cups toddy
¼ tsp salt
4 tbsp crushed jaggery
2 cups freshly grated coconut

- Mix all ingredients, except coconut, to form a thick paste. Cover and leave overnight.

- Next morning, add coconut and mix well. Pour into small metal bowls or an idli steamer and steam for 10 minutes.

- Serve hot or cold.

TANDULACHI BHAKRI

Rice Pancake

Serves 4

250 gm rice flour
1 tsp oil
¼ tsp salt

- Mix all ingredients with water and knead to form firm dough. Make egg-sized balls and set aside.

- Oil palms lightly. Take each ball of dough and press lightly, turning between palms till it forms a palm-sized thick pancake.

- Heat tawa or metal griddle on medium heat. Light another burner on low flame.

- Place bhakri on griddle and cook on both sides, turning it with your hands. When almost done, place bhakri quickly on open flame and turn deftly with your hands, roasting it on both sides.

- Serve hot, with ghee if preferred.

TANDULACHI GOD BHAKRI

Sweet Rice Pancake

Serves 4

250 gm rice flour
4 tbsps jaggery
2 cups grated tadgola (this may be substituted
by freshly grated coconut)
1 tsp oil
¼ tsp salt

- The method of cooking is the same as rice pancake on p. 208.
- These are eaten at breakfast or at teatime.

GODA VARAN

Dal

Serves 4

125 gm tuvar dal
¼ tsp salt
1 tsp oil
1 pinch asafoetida powder
1 tsp turmeric powder

- Boil lentils till very soft, adding water as necessary to form thick soup consistency.

- When cooked, add all other ingredients and cook for 3 minutes.

- Churn mixture in an electric mixture or with a hand blender.

- Serve piping hot with steamed rice.

Glossary

Amboshi	Dried and salted mango slivers
Amchur	Sour dried mango powder
Amsul	Kokum, Indian variety of plum
Aniseed	Saunf
Asafoetida	Hing
Bangda	Mackarel (Substitutes: herring, trout)
Bhakri	Rice or millet pancake
Bhetki	(Substitute: trout)
Bilimb	Star fruit
Boi	(Substitutes: baby mackarel, sardines, grey mullet)
Bombay duck	Bombil (Substitute: lamprey)
Boomla	Belongs to the lamprey family
Bora	Indian fruit of the quince family
Calamaris	Squid
Cardamom	Elaichi
Chapati	Wheat pancake or bread
Chimbori	Crab
Cinammon	Dalchini
Clove	Long

Coconut feni	Cococnut country liquor
Coconut milk	Extracted from freshly grated coconut by blending with water in liquidizer and straining through muslin
Coriander seeds	Dhania
Coriander leaves	Dhania patta
Cottage cheese	Paneer
Cumin	Jeera
Curry leaves	Karipatta
Dal	Lentils
Dhan sakh masala	Mixture of about twenty spices used in making dhan sakh, a Parsi speciality
Dill	Shepoo
Fenugreek	Methi
Garam masala	Mixed aromatic spices
Garlic	Lahsan
Ghee	Clarified butter
Ginger	Adrak
Gol fish	(Substitutes: cod, haddock, red snapper)
Hilsa	(Substitute: large trout)
Jaggery	Gur
Jawla	Tiny prawn
Kakda	Vegetable local to Maharashtra
Kalwa	Oyster
Kane	Lady fish (Substitute: any brackish water fish)
Karandi	Tiny prawn
Karela	Bitter gourd
Kevda essence	Fragrant essence of the kevda plant, akin to rose water

King fish	(Substitute: rawas)
Kolam rice	Very small-grained rice from Maharashtra
Kolambi	Prawn
Koshimbir	Salad with chopped onion, tomatoes, coriander leaves, diced green chillies, sugar, salt and lime juice
Mace	Jaipatri
Mandeli	Anchovy
Modka	Whitebait
Mustard seeds	Sarson
Nutmeg	Jaiphal
Okra	Lady's finger or bhindi
Pomfret	(Substitutes: sole, flounder)
Pulao	Spicy rice
Radish koshimbir	Salad made with grated white radish, curd, diced green chillies, sugar and salt
Rawa	Semolina
Rawas	Rui, rohu (Subsitutes: tuna, red snapper)
Red snapper	Rawas
Roe	Caboli
Seer fish	(Substitute: rawas)
Shevaiya	Spaghetti or vermicelli
Shevala	Vegetable local to Maharashtra
Shevandi	Lobster
Surmai	(Substitute: salmon)
Tadgola	Fruit of toddy palm
Tamarind	Imli
Teesrya	Clam
Toddy	Fermented palm juice
Turmeric	Haldi

Index

Tallelya Kalwavar Ande (Sunny Egg on Oyster), 182-83

CHUTNEYS AND PICKLES

CRAB

CURRIES

HORS D'OEUVRES

PAN-FRIED FISH

PRAWN

SHELLFISH

Double Biya ani Shimpalya (Beans with Mussels), 144-45

Kajutli Kalwan (Oyster in Cashew Cream), 129-30

Kallumakkai (Oyster Pickle), 201

Kalvachey Mulyatley Lonchey (Fresh Oyster and Radish Pickle), 196

Kismis ani Kalwa (Oyster and Sultana Hors D'oeuvre) 186-87

Sahahalyat Kalvey (Oyster Green Masala with Fresh Coconut), 124

Shevaiya ani Shimplya (Spicy Spaghetti and Shellfish), 146-48

Shimplya ani Tomatocha Pulao (Shellfish and Tomato Piquant Pulao), 82-83

Tallelya Kalwavar Ande (Sunny Egg on Oyster), 182-83

SPECIALITY SEAFOOD

Akhya Shahalyatlya Kolambya (Prawns in Whole Coconut), 108-9

Amboshtli Kolambi (Prawn with Amboshi), 127-28

Amli ne Machhi no Patio (Tamarind and Fish Patio), 159-60

Amsul ani Mothi Kolambi (Amsul and King Prawn Stew), 137-38

Amsulatli Wafleli Machhi (Baked Fish with Amsul), 116

Baked Niste (Baked Masala Fish), 150-51

Bhaji ani Kolambicha Stew (Stewed Vegetables with Prawns), 106-7

Bhajlela Saranga (Baked Fish), 89-90

Darutla Saranga (Poached Pomfret in Feni), 131-32

Double Biya ani Shimplya (Beans with Mussels), 144-45